EVERY 1 A WINNER!

BLUE RIBBON RECIPES

By Sue-Ann K. Dondlinger

Suesta

Richfield, Wisconsin

First Edition.

Library of Congress Catalog Number: 94-80028
ISBN: 0-9638825-1-1

Published by
Suesta
2272 Slinger Road
Richfield, Wisconsin 53076

Printed by
Palmer Publications, Inc.
P.O. Box 296
Amherst, Wisconsin 54406

On the Cover

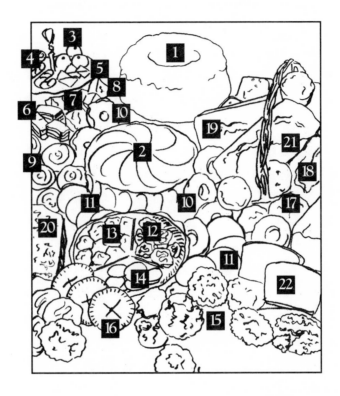

Dedication

Even though I always dreamed of doing so, I could not have put together this special book without the help of many people, not to mention their taste buds and tummies! I give a tremendous thank you to my husband and friend, John, who was not only my sounding board, but a cooperative, if not a some-what captive, sampler of the foods I made! Thanks also to our children, Daniel and Theresa, for tasting any and all of my baked goods and giving me their honest opinions; a very special thank you to my mother, who nurtured this baking fanatic with constant encouragement and help from the beginning. I certainly must express my appreciation to all the other relatives and friends, especially to Mark who helped me with the title. Also, to all those dedicated bakers who I competed with and learned from in fair competition as well as the food competition judges, whose expert advice and comments were of great value. To all who added their "two cents worth" or were the "tasters" of my baking results, I thank you for your "input"! Writing this book has been a most rewarding experience. Yes, dreams can come true!

Sue-Ann K. Corrigan-Dondlinger

TABLE OF CONTENTS

Introduction

Baking is a joy for me and it has become a big part of my life. It is a unique art I learned to love. Yes, I call it an art because I think baking and cooking is a collection of many facets of artistry: an eye for detail, color, size, shape, even a flair for the dramatic, and of course, a certain amount of skill and patience as well. The reward is the special feeling you get when you measure and mix ingredients to create a culinary delight that is not only pleasing to the eye but great on the taste buds!

A lot of work and years of practice brought me from the family kitchen to winning blue ribbons at the Wisconsin State Fair and the Washington County Fair food competitions. There were a number of baking mishaps, a few "flops" but a lot of successes as well along the way.

When I learned to bake over 38 years ago, it was out of necessity, not because it was something to pass the time or because it was the "in" thing to do! I learned from a real pro, my mother. She, in turn, learned much the same way from her mother. She told me many stories of her home and of her mother's baking and cooking for their large Polish family on the farm in North Central Wisconsin. From the time I can remember, my mother always baked for our family and for others as well. She rarely missed baking for church bake sales, school functions, or other social events. At home, she did basic bread baking and then baked all sorts of goodies for our family of seven to enjoy. Holidays always meant a lot of extra baking to make those special holiday treats we all can remember, especially at Christmas time.

My mother truly must have liked to bake because I never got the impression from her that it was a terrible job to be dreaded. Instead, we would work together, and I learned a great deal from her. When I was young, I remember that she always let me help her in the kitchen doing even little things to aid her in baking. I'd find recipes, get the ingredients together for a batch of cookies or a cake, get out the measuring cups and spoons or the right pans, and I learned the most necessary job of all, to clean up the kitchen after a days' baking!

One thing I always wanted to do when I was learning to bake was to use Mom's Sunbeam Mix-Master. The "pride and joy" of her kitchen. This was in the 1950's when electric kitchen mixers were showing up in most kitchens and were THE "state of the art" as far as kitchen equipment went. My mom always told me that, until I knew how to handle the mixer properly, I should never touch it without her around. Well, as a ten-year-old who sort of knew her way around the kitchen, I thought everything should go quickly! So, when I finally did get my hands on her Mix-Master, I'd turn it to the highest speed and watch those beaters move! After all, what was a mixer with a motor for, right? It wasn't until I got a rubber scraper caught between those fast-moving beaters, and it whipped out just inches of my face, that I took heed to what Mom had said! But eventually under Mom's guidance and patience I did learn the proper use of the mixer! This is the key to my love of baking: Mom actually LET ME have the experiences in the kitchen, good or bad!

My dad used to say that too much of a good thing can be bad for you. I remember having just a little too much "free reign" in the kitchen. It happened in the summer when I was ten. My younger brother, Pat, and I, who were closest in age, did our work together at that time. Well, Mom worked outside the home for that summer and Dad was a self-employed carpenter at home. Anyway, Mom left us in charge of making the daily lunches and yes, we could bake some cookies if we were careful and let Dad know what we were up to. So we decided to bake Christmas spritz cookies, using a cookie press, even though it was June. Well, I showed off to my brother by getting the dough mixed up in record-breaking time. The dough just didn't seem right so I added more flour. Then we couldn't get the dough through the cookie press. This simple baking adventure was not going well!

We had the kitchen in such a mess! Dough was scattered on the table, the floor, the counter, half in and half out of the cookie press, and we still hadn't baked any cookies! Finally, Pat said we should make cutout cookies because the dough "kinda" looked like that type of cookie dough. So we did. We could hardly keep the dough together enough to make decent shapes but finally got the pan in the oven. We baked them and let them cool before tasting our handy work. They were awful! So we did what comes naturally to kids—we hid them! Meanwhile, the kitchen was a total disaster, and we knew we better get it cleaned up before Mom came home, which would be real soon because we spent so much time trying to make the cookies! So we got busy and swept up the spilled flour and dough from the floor. I'm not sure if it was my idea or Pat's, but we then decided we better wash the floor as well to remove any tell-tale signs of the messy kitchen. So, to speed things up, we used the kitchen sink spray to get the water onto the tile floor quickly and into all those hard to reach places like under the stove and refrigerator! So much water was on the floor that we had to sop it up with bath towels, which of course, we promptly rolled up in a ball and threw in a laundry basket!

When Mom came home and asked how the cookie baking went, we said that it went just fine and that we ate the cookies. But as she stepped around her kitchen, Mom saw some elusive puddles near the stove. We gave the best answer kids know, we shrugged our shoulders and said, "I don't know." By the next morning the curling corners of the floor tiles and the molding towels gave us away! Then the whole story came out, even the awful cookies came out of hiding. What a lecture we got! I think I washed dishes for a week! After that kitchen fiasco, I was surprised my mother even let me back in the kitchen! But she did, although I had to once again prove I could be responsible in the kitchen! This is only one of many kitchen adventures I had while growing up.

This kind of hands-on experience provided the foundation that helped to pave the way to my blue ribbon baking future. I learned through trial and error and lots of practice! I botched a lot of recipes and made bakery so bad my mom's backyard chickens wouldn't even eat it! But eventually, success covered a multitude of blunders. As years went by, I received a lot of praise for my bakery but passed it off because it didn't seem to me to be such a "big deal" to bake something—it was routine for me. My mother and others kept complimenting me on how good my bakery was and kept encouraging me to continue baking even though I was very busy with husband, family, and part-time job. It was sometimes difficult to do ANY baking at all!

In 1972, a good friend of mine, Judy, gave me the last push to enter the state fair baking competition. She came over for lunch and again complimented me on how well I baked. During this visit, she was very insistent about me entering into competition because some of her friends entered the state fair, won ribbons, and had fun. Finally, I called for information. I received that year's Premium Book and an entry form, and I ended up entering one thing, a frosted orange drop cookie. I put twelve cookies on a paper plate, packed the kids in the car, drove down to state fair park, handed the cookies in, and left. We went to the fair the following weekend, and I saw my cookies. I had won a second place red ribbon! Needless to say, I was overjoyed. I hadn't realized then how difficult it was to win ANY ribbon at the state fair because of all the competition and "exactness" involved.

At state and county fair competitions, not only the finest quality and taste are judged, but rules have to be followed exactly as printed in the Premium Book. It is necessary to be this precise for the judges to choose the top four winning places from as many as 100 entries in one category! It often is a very difficult task and the judges have said themselves that it is necessary to eliminate very good products. Even the simplest thing as having 13 cookies on a plate instead of 12 would mean disqualification! Sometimes it comes down to the size of pieces that fruit has been cut into or the grating size of cheese that can bring one entry up above the others. Size, color, texture, weight, smell, appearance, and taste are all elements used by judges to arrive at their final decisions. Many of the entries would probably get a ribbon but there is a limit of four placings for each category! However, if in the judge's opinion there isn't the best quality product among those being judged, they do not have to, nor do they always, give a placing. It is rare but they are looking for the best they can find! This is the great difference in baking for the family table and baking for competition. What you make may taste excellent, but it has to also look, smell, and feel perfect!

After the first year, I also learned you could stay and watch the state fair judging and get first-hand comments and advice about the entries being judged. So, the next year, I baked several kinds of cookies, again packed up the two kids, and headed for the State Fair Park in West Allis. I started to "learn the ropes." I realized if you wanted to watch the judging later, you had to secure a seat right away, so getting there when the doors opened was the best time. Each entrant received a number, and when your number was called, you submitted your food entries. Sometimes this took several hours. I would settle my two children on chairs with their coloring books, crayons, story books, our bagged lunch, and other paraphernalia and wait my turn to submit my entries. As it was a long day for them, the children were then taken home before judging started.

At county fairs, the number of categories to enter are often limited and the number of entrants in each category is less. This is a great place to hear a judge's comments and advice. Listen well and take notes because all that you hear at the county fair judging can be used to help you win ribbons at any level! I was very fortunate to have an excellent county fair judge. For years I have sat with others at the food judging, writing down her remarks, criticisms, and other observations. Her instructions and advice (as well as those from all the judges) encouraged me to become an improved baker, to achieve ribbons, and make every one a winner!

In my early years of competition at the state fair, judging rarely started on time, but when it did, it usually continued on into the late night hours. One year the final item was not judged until 11:40 PM! As most of us arrived as early as 8:30 AM, this became a very long day.

Over the last 20 years, a number of improvements have been made to make learning from and winning at the fair easier. Processing of entries has become more efficient. Now judging usually occurs pretty much on schedule with very few breaks. The butter, honey, cheese, and apple categories always seemed to take more time for judging and when more and more specialty categories sponsored by cookie, shortening, cake flour, yeast, and canning companies were added, the judging was divided between two days: one day for basic entries and another devoted entirely to judging of special categories. Some companies have representatives there to award the winners their prizes. Also, photographers and reporters are there to write articles for the food sections of newspapers. Dividing the food judging competition between two days does justice to all the entrants.

One of the most welcomed improvements was air conditioning in the Family Living Center, which helped to keep the heat and humidity from making a disaster of the prize food entries. Also, the production of plastic and disposable containers made our task of storing and carrying top quality products to the fair a lot easier.

Even with these improvements and with careful preparations and handling of entries, there is one thing each winner competes against and does not win—and that is time! The food judging for the state fair takes place anywhere from four to seven days before the state fair EVEN OPENS!! Then the winning items are displayed for the length of the fair. So, by the tenth and final day of the fair, no matter how excellent your entry appeared at the judging time, it really does not look very appealing! While most county fairs are open for a shorter time, the limited space and, in almost all cases, lack of refrigeration, keep the winning entries from looking their best as well. So, when you are at the fair and hear someone comment about how the winning entries look, think of us and the "time-factor"!

There is a very special feeling I get when I think of the yearly fair competition. Before fair time, the family left me alone to "do my thing"! On the days of baking, they knew to "tip-toe" softly and not disturb my kitchen area! It is a time of "good" stress and a time of creativity! SO, here I am creating, making a thorough mess of my kitchen, and getting carry-out food for supper! But unless you bake for competition, you can't fully understand this creative madness that takes over! When you practice and bake for the fair competition, you are trying to make the best that you can, even if it means making a product repeatedly. You take your creations with high hopes of getting that recognition of a "job well done."

But as with any other competition, you must keep it in perspective. Many competitors consider this very serious business and will do everything possible to win. I compete for the pure joy and satisfaction it gives me to create. If I don't win in a category, I try again or maybe not, it depends on how I feel about the category. Sometimes, after not placing in a category, I will enter it again until I personally achieve my goal and make the product the best I can, whether I win or not.

When you enter your products in fair competition, you seek approval from not only the judges but from a large group of some of the best cooks and bakers in the state! We are all dedicated to trying to do the best we can. One of the unique results of competition at the fairs is the many, many friends I have made through the years. We all bring our coolers with our lunches, seat cushions for comfort, thermos bottles for a coffee break, and something to snack on as we settle in for the long hours of judging. We renew acquaintances and make new friends. And as we all sit together, we listen attentively to what the judges tell us and the reasons why they chose one entry over the other. We all wait anxiously to see our foods judged, but we ban together to cheer and praise each other for a good job, whether it's for fourth, third, second or first place. There are no "rejects"! It's the camaraderie that keeps me coming back each year. I have made friendships with these talented people even though we only spend a few days out of the year together or send short notes during the year. We belong to a very special, dedicated group that is ever growing. So many different people, men, women, and teens, from a variety of occupations enjoy competing at fair time. All of us "old-timers" welcome the new faces who come each year and bring their "best." It's good to see so many people returning to the art of baking and cooking and obviously enjoying it!

As I took our children with me to the competition, it seemed only natural that they would start baking. Our daughter, Theresa, soon was banging around the family kitchen. I let her have the experiences of doing the work herself and she found what fun baking could be! She first entered in the Washington County Fair at the age of ten years. Soon after, as she won ribbons and became more skilled, it was no surprise that she was entering open class competitions at the Wisconsin State Fair and winning blue ribbons there as well! After college, she married Chris and they have a daughter Hannah. She certainly has limited time now but perhaps she will compete again some day, and maybe take *her* daughter along!

Our son, Dan, works well in the kitchen but he really didn't have a chance to show what he could do with Terri and me taking over the kitchen most of the time! It wasn't until he was in college that he showed his hidden talent for baking, among other things, very good yeast bread products! He is married to Denise and perhaps he'll share this talent with his son, John Daniel.

I have always loved to bake and entering in competition is one of my special hobbies. Like anything else, it takes some hard work, a touch of talent and a little "elbow grease" to accomplish, but it sure is worth it! I proudly display in my kitchen all the fair ribbons that I have won in over 22 years of competition. Usually after winning a ribbon place in a category, I did not enter the same recipe again to try to win a blue ribbon; I would look for a better recipe. If I did win a blue ribbon for a product I made, I did not enter that same recipe to try to win another blue ribbon for the same thing the next year. There are so many wonderful recipes to try and new challenges that I was always trying something new! Besides, once you have achieved the goal of a blue ribbon, you have already proven to be the best in that category, so why do it again!

This book contains blue-ribbon-winning recipes that I have tested and developed in my own kitchen and entered in county and state fair competition. All the recipes are from my personal collection; some have been gathered from many different people and places and some I have developed myself. Next to each recipe you'll see a ribbon with the year in which I won for that product. Some recipes also won gold excellence ribbons; these recipes received the honor of being the best in the Washington County open class food judging for that year. In addition, there is information that I've collected over the years to help you if you are considering entering into fair competition or if you just want to bake for your family.

To win any of the four place ribbons in fair food competition is a great achievement, and after you compete for years, you realize just how special they are! It took me a few years and winning many second places and a few third and fourth place ribbons before I won my first blue ribbon at the state fair competition. You will have "flops" or mishaps and you may not win anything the first time you enter, but keep trying. Whatever the difficulties you may encounter, nothing compares to the satisfaction you feel reaching this personal achievement of competing with so many good bakers and winning a ribbon at the county or state fair! You may compete against as few as a dozen entries in some categories and as many as seventy-five or more entries in the specialty categories. You can be very proud of yourself just for entering!

But to enter into fair competition is hard work! The key to being good at anything, including baking and cooking, is practice! You should look for the best ways to improve both the preparation technique and the taste quality of your product. Once you find a recipe or develop one, practice making it until you have the best you can reproduce. Of course, as any good cook or baker will tell you, no two products made from the same recipe will be identical as we each have a baking style and flair of our own. Following basic procedures and using basic skills, however, are a "must" for producing a good end product.

To find out where and when your county fair is held, the best place to start is with the county seat offices. Call the fair directors' office to get necessary information for entering. An entry form and Premium Book are sent upon request. Call the state fair directors' office to find out the information you need to enter the state level of food competition. The fair offices welcome phone calls to answer any questions you might have but follow the directions in the Premium Book EXACTLY and you'll soon be on your way to competing!

So what are you waiting for? Start baking! Be creative, have fun, and make every one a winner!

COOKIES

COOKIES

The first category I'd like to introduce to you is my favorite —cookies! The very first ribbon I won in fair competition was for cookies. I was thrilled! Any cookie is indeed a work of art, a unique creation carefully cut out or molded to just the right size, and decorated any way you'd like. It is also a most versatile gift, especially at Christmas time. When you make them, it becomes a special gift just from you, and it is certainly a gift gratefully accepted by all. In addition, according to any child, a cookie saves them from after school "starvation" or when they feel they just can not survive without some form of food before supper is served!

For me, cookies are the most fun to bake because there are SO many variations to choose from. Most families have their favorites, but I think chocolate chip cookies top the list, especially when they are right from the oven and the chocolate chips are still warm and "gooey" and oh so good! But there are many of kinds of rolled, molded, pressed, dropped, and bar cookie recipes that you can enjoy making.

Cookies were the first bakery I attempted to make when I was young. I remember one of the first batches of cookies that I made all by myself when I was about nine years old. I thought I did everything the way my mom taught me. I read the recipe, the method, gathered all the ingredients, used the mixer to blend it all together, then I baked them. After taking them out of the oven and cooling them, I stacked them on a plate to offer them to my family as dessert. Well, my dad, bless his Irish heart, took one of the odd little balls and eyed it long and carefully. To my horror he then proceeded to tap it on the edge of his saucer. When this rock-hard lump, posing as a cookie, wouldn't even dent, he dunked it in his tea saying very straight faced, "Well, they are solid, but tea softens them up a bit." My brothers were not as kind; they were practically rolling on the floor in laughter at the sorry sight of those cookies! But I wouldn't be stopped, and I made sure the next batch of cookies was better each time after that. To this day, if I make a batch of cookies that does not turn out exactly right, I think back to when I first tried my hand at making cookies and have to smile. Now many years later, my brothers don't seem to mind eating my cookies, especially at Christmas time!

It seems I was always baking cookies, whether it was for bake sales, gifts, parties, or the cookie jar. I was fortunate enough to be employed only during the school day hours, so I was able to be there when our children came home from school. One of the after school treats I tried to provide for them was freshly baked homemade cookies, still hot from the oven. I am usually experimenting with some kind of cookie dough and take cookies whenever I go to the dentist or doctor's office and as treats for my work or my husband's job site.

The best recipe I produced was for a cookie I entered in the 1993 Archway Cookie Company's contest at the Wisconsin State Fair and won the first prize and their award. I tried for years and after coming close many times, I finally succeeded and reached my secret goal of winning this cookie contest!

MY TIPS FOR BAKING

Anywhere in this book when a recipe calls for flour, use the following procedure: using all-purpose flour, unless noted otherwise, scoop flour into measuring cup, then take a table knife and level off the top. Sift flour when recipe suggests and use cake flour if stated. Always follow the recipe carefully.

When margarine is called for, use regular stick margarine.

Remember there are two kinds of measuring cups. The one to measure dry ingredients has NO rim; the top of the cup is the measure line. If you try to use these cups for liquid, filling them to the rim, you would probably spill some of it and then your measurement would not be right. A glass or clear cup is used for liquid measurement as the measuring marks are below the rim of the cup so you can measure without spilling. Remember to always measure accurately.

MY TIPS FOR BAKING COOKIES

1. Read the recipe very carefully! Make sure you have the ingredients on hand before you begin. For those who bake often, this is not a problem, but if you do not bake often, check your supplies. Use only fresh baking soda and baking powder. Also check your spices and nuts to make sure they are fresh. Fair competition requires the highest quality ingredients to produce the best product.

2. After reading the recipe, gather together all the ingredients and baking utensils you will need.

3. Re-read the recipe, then prepare the dough. Never guess—measure the ingredients for your recipe very carefully. Do not change amounts of such basic ingredients as flour, sugar, liquid, or shortening; use no more or less than the recipe states. It sure makes a difference in the end product, especially when baking for the fair.

4. To prepare the baking sheets, coat lightly with spray shortening. Be careful not to spray too much as the cookies may scorch. Non-stick pans are OK, but sometimes they tend to brown the cookies more than you want. The insulated pans are great, but remember the cookies will continue to bake on these pans because they retain their heat longer. Once the pan is out of the oven, don't leave the cookies on the pan to cool, remove immediately. The advantage of using these insulated pans is that they bake and brown evenly.

5. Heat oven to the proper temperature for your cookies. Pre-heat your oven according to manufacturer's directions and allow enough time for the oven to reach that temperature. Buy a good oven thermometer so you can determine how your oven is heating. Watch your oven temperature and timing closely.

6. After the baking sheet has been prepared, the oven preheated, and the dough mixed, you may want to make a test cookie, especially if you're working on a recipe for competition. Place dough for one cookie on the baking sheet. Once baked, you'll be able to see if the dough needs to be chilled, if more flour should be added, or if other adjustments need to be made. With practice, you'll be able to tell what the dough needs.

7. For competition, you'll want to make the cookies as equal in size as you can get because you will need twelve identical cookies. The cookies must be baked alike top and bottom. Bake all twelve cookies on the same pan to achieve this consistent browning. Don't mix groups of twelve as the judge will be able to tell they weren't baked together, and you will be able to see the difference too with practice. Bake cookies for fair competition one sheet of cookies at a time, placed on an oven rack in the center of the oven. If you are baking two sheets at a time, place racks so they divide oven into thirds. Remember, the recipe states to bake your cookies, or any product for that matter, a certain amount of time. When the least amount of time is up, check to see if your cookies are done. Ovens vary in baking so watch closely.

8. Take cookies from the oven and let cool one minute on the baking sheet. Carefully remove the cookies and let cool completely. Don't cool cookies in a draft as cookies could shrink and be misshapen.

MY TIPS FOR MAKING HONEY COOKIES

1. It is always good to use a recipe adapted for honey, but you can substitute honey for sugar in your own recipe by using equal amounts of honey for sugar up to one cup, then reduce the total amount of other liquids by one quarter cup for every cup of honey used.

2. Light colored honey, like clover honey, is usually mild in flavor. If you have honey that is dark and has a heavier taste, add 1/4 teaspoon baking soda for each cup of honey in baking as this will help neutralize honey's natural acidity.

3. Rinse the measuring cup with warm water or coat it with spray shortening before measuring the honey. This makes it easier to pour out of the cup.

4. Honey not only sweetens but adds body and a delicate flavor to many products. In fact, goods sweetened with honey seem to taste even better the day after they are baked! Remember when making a dough mixture, add honey in a fine stream while beating. This adds volume to the batter. Honey helps give a moist, tender texture to breads, cakes, cookies, and other baked goods and helps them stay fresh.

5. If using honey in a recipe that calls for sugar, lower the oven temperature about 25 degrees because honey browns faster than sugar. If your recipe is adapted for honey, the oven temperature given should be correct. In any case, watch your oven closely when baking with honey.

6. To store honey, keep in a dry place at room temperature so it does not absorb moisture. All honey granulates with time, but that doesn't affect its taste at all. If honey granulates, just place the open container in a pan of warm water until it's liquid again, or microwave uncovered on high about one minute.

MY TIPS FOR MAKING DROP COOKIES

The easiest of all cookies is the drop cookie. This versatile cookie can be made flavorful by using juices instead of milk or by adding chocolate chips, nuts, or fruit. Drop cookies are quick and easy when baking for your family, BUT when baking them for competition, it takes a little more "doing"!

1. Prepare dough according to recipe. If the kitchen is warm, chill dough before baking so drop cookies do not spread.

2. Make sure baking sheets are cold before putting the next batch of cookie dough on them; hot baking sheets can also cause cookies to spread.

3. Drop dough by spoonfuls onto a prepared baking sheet, about 2 inches apart, to make a $2^1/_2$-inch round cookie.

4. Bake cookies at temperature stated in recipe. Watch cookies closely. Cookies should be slightly rounded and of uniform shape and color. The bottom of a well-baked drop cookie, like chocolate chip or oatmeal, should look similar in color to the top. Overbaking could lead to dry, hard cookies with dark crusty edges. Underbaked cookies will be doughy.

MY TIPS FOR MAKING ROLLED COOKIES

Besides the rolled molasses cutout cookies, white sugar cookies are probably the best known rolled cookies. It's usually the first kind of cookie a small child is given to eat. Well-made rolled cookies should have a good shape of the cutter, be lightly browned on top, crisp or soft depending on the thickness, and have a delicate flavor. White sugar cookies are plain and simple and do not have a lot of extra ingredients added.

My Grandma Torzewski probably made her sugar cookies with a "spoon of butter, a scoop of sugar, and two handfuls of flour"! Like most hard-working farm women in the early 1900's, she knew her measuring system for baking so well that only eyesight and touch were necessary. The women didn't have a lot of time to waste, so they learned their skills quickly and thoroughly! According to my mom, her mother's cookies were always great tasting. My grandma baked cookies with what my mother remembers her calling "hearts-horn," which was purchased at the drugstore in the 1920's and probably was a brand name for a type of baking powder or cream of tartar. They would use it especially in the summer to keep cookies crisp.

Cutting out sugar cookies in special shapes is probably something we all remember fondly, whether it was for Christmas with shapes of stars, bells, angels, camels, santas, and trees, or Easter shapes of bunnies and chicks. Many other shapes are appropriate throughout the year: hearts, shamrocks, turkeys, and pumpkins.

1. Chill dough about one hour after mixing and then use only about one-third of the dough at a time.

2. Don't use a lot of flour; just sprinkle the cutting board lightly and rub some on the rolling pin. The more extra flour you roll into the dough, the tougher your cookies will be.

3. Roll dough out evenly and the cookies will bake evenly. For a thin and crispy cookie, roll dough thin; for a thick and soft cookie, roll dough thicker. Dip cookie cutter in flour and shake off extra flour. Cut the shapes close together so the dough won't have to be re-rolled as often.

4. To make a shape without a cutter, simply cut the shape out of cardboard. Then grease the cardboard and lay it on the rolled out dough. Cut around cardboard with a sharp knife and "presto," the cookie shape desired!

5. Time does not always permit the fun of using cutters, so you may use a "quick method" of making sugar cookies. Simply form balls of dough the size of walnuts and place on a cookie sheet. Dip flat-bottomed glass in granulated sugar and press down each ball. My sister, Marion, used to say I cheated when making sugar cookies like this, but it's an easy way to get the great taste of rolled sugar cookies.

6. Lift cutout cookies from board to the cookie sheet with care. Watch cookies as they bake, and bake for the least amount of time the recipe states so they are baked just right. Especially watch thinner cookies because they will burn very easily! Let cookies set for about 1 minute on cookie sheet before removing them to cool.

7. The last scraps of dough that have perhaps been rolled several times can still be used. At Christmas, use this dough to cut out Christmas shapes to later decorate and hang on the tree. After Christmas, hang old cookies on an outside tree to give the birds a great winter treat!

MY TIPS FOR MAKING MOLDED COOKIES

Probably the most familiar molded cookies are the traditional peanut butter cookies that are crisscrossed on top with a fork. Christmas pecan fingers are another favorite that take a lot of patience and time to mold, but the results are very rewarding.

1. Make dough as the recipe directs. Most recipes require you to chill the dough well before shaping. Chilling this rich dough first makes it easier to handle. Roll dough in your palms to make it smooth. The smoother it is the more evenly the cookie will brown.

2. When making crescents, candy canes, or balls, take time to mold cookies carefully so they are of equal size and shape. Don't make cookies too large.

MY TIPS FOR MAKING PRESSED COOKIES

1. Use a good recipe for pressed cookies and remember to chill the dough because this type of dough has a lot of butter in it. You need to chill dough so you can work with it easily; however, chilling it too long can make it dry and crumbly.

2. Work with only a small amount of dough at a time. Force dough through cookie press, in the desired shape, onto an ungreased, cold baking sheet.

3. Be sure your baking sheet is cold. If baking sheets are too warm, fat in the dough will break down, start to melt, and the cookies will pull away from the sheet when cookie press is lifted.

4. Bake until cookie is set and just delicately browned. A well-made pressed cookie will also have a good shape and a nice buttery flavor.

MY TIPS FOR MAKING BAR COOKIES

The best known and loved bar cookie is the brownie. Brownies became famous in the late 1930's and legend has it that the first brownies were a fallen chocolate cake! However it happened, they sure are a favorite and easy to make. Brownies have a rich, moist quality with just a very thin crust on top and have a great chocolate flavor.

1. Follow the recipe or be creative here. Use a basic bar cookie recipe but make your own variations, using M & M's, marshmallows, or different nuts.

2. Spread dough in greased square or oblong pan and bake in a preheated oven, checking at the minimum amount of baking time.

3. Watch bars closely. Test for doneness on a fudgey-type bar by baking until top has a dull crust. Bake cake-like bars until a wooden pick inserted in center comes out clean, and bake meringue-topped bars until delicately browned.

4. If you frost bars or brownies, wait until completely cold, then frost with a thin, chocolate glaze rather than a heavy frosting.

5. To make a good looking brownie or any other bar cookie, make sure you use a sharp knife and cut bars into equal pieces with clean cut sides. For fair competition, bars are to be cut into one-inch by three-inch bars. When baking bars for your family, cut them any size you wish. Any way you cut them, they are an easy and quick cookie to make.

MY TIPS FOR STORING COOKIES

1. To store soft cookies, place in container with a tight cover. Also store bar cookies tightly covered.

2. To store crisp cookies, place in container with loose fitting cover. If they soften, as sometimes they can, especially in humid weather, heat oven to 300 degrees and place on baking sheet for about 3 to 5 minutes to crisp them up.

3. When freezing cookies, remember that all baked cookies freeze well except for meringue types or those that have filling. Baked cookies can be kept in the freezer at 0 degrees or lower for a maximum of six months. I do much of my Christmas cookie baking early and take advantage of my large freezer to store the cookies. Make sure to pack them tightly so they remain fresh. Then, when it is close to Christmas, take out those cookies that need frosting and spend time on the details of decorating. Freezing most of the cookies also gives you extra time to make spe-

cialty cookies that require a lot of time. Defrost your cookies in unopened packages to keep them from softening. You can also freeze refrigerator cookie dough to take out, slice, and bake cookies as needed. I also found you can freeze regular cookie dough especially when you have time to mix the dough but no time to bake cookies. After mixing, just put in tightly covered container. Thaw in refrigerator before baking.

I DO NOT recommend baking and freezing of cookies to be used in fair competition; they simply are not the best quality.

MY TIPS FOR MAILING COOKIES

1. Choose cookies that will travel well and can be handled roughly like crinkles, most kinds of drop cookies, brownies (unfrosted) and other bar-type cookies, most refrigerator cookies, and filled cookies. Regular cookies or bar cookies that have a lot of fruit in them will stay soft. Thin and crisp cookies are great tasting but not good to send because they break too easily.

2. When sending cookies, use a tin or sturdy plastic container. First line the container with wax paper. It works better to pack heavier cookies, especially the bar cookies, on the bottom and place layers of lighter cookies on top with wax paper in between. Make sure you put more crumpled wax paper directly on top of cookies before you put the lid on.

3. Tape a card with neatly printed address to top of cookie container. Place container in box, using either paper or popped popcorn as packing material. Fill all corners so container won't move when handled. Tape box closed, print address and return address, and cover with clear packing tape.

CHEWIES

1993 Winner of Archway Cookie Contest
Wisconsin State Fair

1	cup margarine, softened	2	cups flour
3/4	cup granulated sugar	2	teaspoons baking powder
1¼	cups brown sugar, packed	1½	teaspoons cinnamon
1½	tablespoons molasses	3/4	teaspoon salt
2½	teaspoons maple extract	2	cups quick oatmeal
2	eggs	2¼	cups crisp rice cereal

Beat margarine and sugars until light and fluffy. Add molasses, maple extract, and eggs. Mix well. Add flour, baking powder, cinnamon, and salt. Blend well. If dough is too soft, chill 1 hour. Stir in oatmeal and cereal. Drop by heaping spoonfuls formed into round balls 2 inches apart on a greased cookie sheet. Bake in 350-degree oven until light brown, 8 to 10 minutes. Do not overbake! Cool on cookie sheets about 1 minute, then remove to cooling rack to cool completely.

Makes 5 to 5½ dozen cookies.

Featured on the cover.

CHOCOLATE DROPS

1/2	cup margarine, softened
1	cup sugar
1	egg
2	ounces unsweetened chocolate, melted and cooled
3/4	cup sour milk
11/4	teaspoons vanilla
13/4	cups flour
1/4	teaspoon salt
1/2	teaspoon baking soda
3/4	cup chopped nuts, optional

Chocolate Frosting:

1	tablespoon margarine
1	ounce unsweetened chocolate
1	cup powdered sugar
2	tablespoons warm water

To make cookies, cream margarine and sugar until light and fluffy. Beat in egg, then cooled chocolate. Stir in sour milk and vanilla. Add flour, salt, and baking soda. Stir in nuts. Chill the dough at least 1 hour. Drop by heaping teaspoonfuls on a lightly greased cookie sheet. Place about 2 inches apart. Bake in 350-degree oven for 8 to 10 minutes or until no imprint stays when you touch the top. Cool completely before frosting cookies.

To make chocolate frosting, in the microwave or over low heat, melt margarine and unsweetened chocolate. Add powdered sugar and warm water. Stir until smooth and easy to spread, adding a few extra drops of water if necessary. Frost cookies.

Makes about 4 dozen cookies.

Featured on the cover.

1987

CHOCOLATE HONEY COOKIES

1	cup margarine	2$1/2$	cups flour
1$1/4$	cups honey	1	teaspoon baking powder
2	eggs, beaten	$1/2$	teaspoon salt
2	ounces unsweetened chocolate, melted and cooled	1	teaspoon cinnamon
		1$1/2$	cups oatmeal
		1	cup chopped pecans

Cream margarine well and add honey in a fine stream. Add beaten eggs and cooled chocolate and mix well. Add dry ingredients. Stir in pecans. Drop by teaspoonfuls 2 inches apart onto lightly greased cookie sheet. Bake in 325-degree oven for 10 to 12 minutes. Remove from pan and cool completely.

Makes 3$1/2$ to 4 dozen cookies.

1984

HONEY SESAME SEED COOKIES

$1/2$	cup butter	$1/2$	teaspoon baking soda
1	cup honey	$1/4$	teaspoon salt
1$1/2$	teaspoons vanilla	1	cup oatmeal
$1/4$	cup wheat germ	$1/4$	cup toasted sesame seeds
1	cup flour	$1/4$	cup dried currants

Cream butter and add honey in a fine stream. Add vanilla. Stir in wheat germ, flour, baking soda, and salt. Blend in oatmeal and stir in sesame seeds. Add currants. Drop by heaping teaspoonfuls 2 inches apart onto lightly greased cookie sheet. Bake in 350-degree oven for 8 to 10 minutes.

Makes 3$1/2$ dozen cookies.

GOLDEN HONEY DROPS

1/2	cup butter	2	teaspoons baking soda
1	cup honey	1	teaspoon salt
3	eggs, well beaten	1	cup chopped pecans
4	cups flour		

Cream butter and add honey in a fine stream. Add eggs and beat well. Add flour, baking soda, and salt. Mix in pecans last. Drop by teaspoonfuls 2 inches apart onto greased cookie sheet and flatten with spoon dipped in warm water. Cookies should be about 1/2-inch thick. Bake in 375-degree oven for 8 to 10 minutes or until golden brown. WATCH closely! Remove from cookie sheet immediately and cool completely.

Makes 6 1/2 to 7 dozen cookies.

PEANUT BUTTER HONEY COOKIES

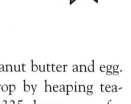

1/2	cup margarine	1 1/4	cups flour
1	cup honey	1/2	teaspoon baking soda
1/2	cup peanut butter	1/2	teaspoon salt
1	egg		

Beat margarine and add honey in a fine stream. Beat in peanut butter and egg. Continue beating until fluffy. Stir in dry ingredients. Drop by heaping tea-spoonfuls 2 inches apart onto greased cookie sheet. Bake in 325-degree oven for 10 to 12 minutes or until nicely browned.

Makes 2 1/2 to 3 dozen cookies.

HONEY ORANGE CHIPPERS

1/2	cup butter	11/4	cups flour
1/2	cup honey	1/2	teaspoon baking soda
1	egg	1/2	teaspoon salt
1	tablespoon grated orange rind	1/3	cup mini chocolate chips
1	teaspoon orange extract	1/3	cup chopped walnuts or other nuts

Cream butter and add honey in a fine stream. Beat in egg, orange rind, and extract. Add flour, baking soda, and salt; then add chocolate chips and nuts. Chill for 30 minutes. Drop by teaspoonfuls 2 inches apart onto lightly greased cookie sheet. Bake in a 350-degree oven for 8 to 10 minutes or until golden brown.

Makes 3 dozen cookies.

HONEY CHERRY BITES

1/2	cup margarine	1/4	teaspoon salt
1	cup honey	1/4	teaspoon cinnamon
1	egg	1	cup oatmeal
1/4	teaspoon almond extract	1/4	cup chopped pecans
11/4	cups flour	1/4	cup chopped and well-drained maraschino cherries
1/2	teaspoon baking soda		

Cream margarine and add honey in a fine stream. Beat in egg and extract. Blend in flour, baking soda, salt, and cinnamon. Stir in oatmeal, pecans, and cherry pieces. Chill 1 hour. Drop by teaspoonfuls 2 inches apart onto lightly greased cookie sheet. Bake in 350-degree oven for 10 to 12 minutes.

Makes 3 to 31/2 dozen cookies.

HONEY RAISIN COOKIES

1/2	cup butter		1/2	teaspoon baking soda
1	cup honey		1	teaspoon salt
1/2	cup sour cream		1	cup oatmeal
2	teaspoons vanilla		1	cup chopped walnuts
2	cups flour		2	cups raisins
1/2	teaspoon baking powder			

Cream butter and add honey in a fine stream. Stir in sour cream and vanilla. Blend in flour, baking powder, baking soda, and salt. Stir in oatmeal, walnuts, and raisins. Chill dough for 30 minutes. Drop by tablespoonfuls onto greased cookie sheet. Bake in 325-degree oven for 12 to 15 minutes or until lightly browned. Let stand for 1 minute on cookie sheet, then remove to wire racks to cool completely.

Makes 3 to 3 1/2 dozen cookies.

HONEY FRUIT DROPS

2	tablespoons orange juice	1$1/4$	cups whole wheat flour
$1/2$	cup chopped dates	$1/4$	teaspoon baking soda
$1/4$	cup margarine	$1/4$	teaspoon salt
$1/2$	cup honey	$1/2$	teaspoon cinnamon
1	small egg	$1/3$	cup chopped pecans
$1/2$	teaspoon orange extract	$1/4$	cup flaked coconut

Pour orange juice over dates and let stand 5 minutes. Cream margarine and add honey in a fine stream. Beat in egg and extract. Blend in flour, baking soda, salt, and cinnamon. Mix in dates with orange juice, pecans, and coconut. Chill 1 hour. Drop by spoonfuls, formed into balls, 2 inches apart onto a greased baking sheet. Flatten balls slightly with fingers. Bake in 350-degree oven for 10 to 12 minutes until light golden brown.

Makes 2$1/2$ to 3 dozen cookies.

HOLIDAY HONEY FRUIT DROPS

1/2	cup margarine	1/2	cup oatmeal
1/2	cup honey	1/2	cup chopped walnuts
1	egg	1/2	cup dried currants
1	teaspoon vanilla	1/2	cup mini chocolate chips
1	cup flour		Red and green sugar for
1	teaspoon baking powder		sprinkling on top
1/4	teaspoon salt		

Cream margarine and add honey in a fine stream. Add egg and vanilla. Stir in flour, baking powder, and salt. Mix in oatmeal, walnuts, currants, and chocolate chips. Chill 1 hour. Drop by heaping teaspoonfuls 2 inches apart onto greased cookie sheet. Sprinkle each cookie with red and green sugar and bake in 350-degree oven for 8 to 10 minutes or until golden brown.

I use this for one of my Christmas cookies. You can eliminate colored sugars for a plain honey cookie.

Makes 31/2 to 4 dozen cookies.

Apricot Honey Drops

Cookies:
- 1/2 cup margarine
- 2/3 cup honey
- 1 teaspoon orange rind
- 1/2 teaspoon orange extract
- 1 cup quick oatmeal
- 1 1/4 cups flour
- 1/2 teaspoon baking soda
- 1/4 teaspoon salt

Apricot Filling:
- 1/4 cup boiling water
- 1/4 cup finely chopped apricots
- 1/4 cup honey
- 1/4 cup finely chopped nuts

To make cookies, cream margarine and add honey in a fine stream. Add orange rind and extract. Blend in dry ingredients. Chill dough 1 hour. Drop by heaping teaspoonfuls 2 inches apart onto greased cookie sheet. Indent center with back of spoon and fill with 1/4 teaspoon apricot filling. Top with 1/4 teaspoon dough. Bake in 350-degree oven for 10 to 12 minutes or until golden brown.

To make filling, pour boiling water over chopped apricots. Let stand 15 minutes. Add honey and chopped nuts and mix well. Let cool before using as filling in cookies.

Makes 2 1/2 to 3 dozen cookies.

WESOLYCH SWIAT-POLISH PRUNE FINGERS

1	pound medium prunes	1	cup dry cottage cheese
	Water to cover prunes	2	cups sifted flour
1	tablespoon sugar	1	cup (approximately)
1	cup butter		powdered sugar

Cover prunes with water and add sugar. Cook until tender and then drain well, cool, and pit. Cut butter and cottage cheese into flour with a pastry blender until a soft dough is formed. Roll dough 1/8-inch thick on floured board and cut into 3-inch squares. Place a cooked prune on each square. Shape dough around prune to resemble a finger and then pinch edges to seal. Place 2 inches apart onto ungreased cookie sheet. Bake at 375 degrees 15 to 18 minutes. Roll in powdered sugar while warm.

Makes 3 to 3 1/2 dozen cookies.

1992

Chocolate Filled Sandwich Cookies

Cookies:
1/2	cup margarine, softened
1/2	cup sugar
1/2	cup brown sugar, packed
1	egg
1/2	teaspoon vanilla
1	cup flour
1/2	teaspoon baking soda
1/4	teaspoon salt
1	cup crushed cornflakes
1	cup oatmeal
1/2	cup flaked coconut

Chocolate Filling:
1	cup semi-sweet chocolate chips
1/2	cup powdered sugar
1	tablespoon hot water
1	teaspoon vanilla
1	3-ounce package cream cheese, at room temperature

To make cookies, cream margarine and sugars until light and fluffy. Beat in egg and vanilla. Blend in dry ingredients, cornflakes, oatmeal, and coconut. Shape dough into 1-inch balls and flatten with bottom of glass dipped in flour. Bake on greased cookie sheet in 350-degree oven for 8 to 10 minutes. Cool.

To make chocolate filling, melt semi-sweet chocolate chips over low heat. With an electric mixer, beat melted chips, powdered sugar, hot water, vanilla, and cream cheese. Blend until smooth, adding a few more drops of water if necessary. Put cookies together bottom to bottom with chocolate filling.

Makes 4 1/2 to 5 dozen sandwich cookies.

PINEAPPLE FILLED COOKIES

Cookies:
- 1/2 cup margarine, softened
- 1 cup sugar
- 2 medium eggs
- 1 1/4 teaspoons vanilla
- 2 1/2 cups flour
- 1/4 teaspoon baking soda
- 1/4 teaspoon salt

Pineapple Filling:
- 1/2 cup sugar
- 2 tablespoons flour
- 3/4 cup crushed pineapple, drained, reserve 6 tablespoons juice
- 1 1/2 tablespoons margarine
- 1/8 teaspoon nutmeg

To make cookies, beat margarine and sugar until fluffy. Stir in eggs and vanilla. Add flour along with baking soda and salt. Blend well. Chill about 2 hours. Roll dough to 1/8-inch thick on floured board. Cut 3-inch rounds and place on lightly greased cookie sheet. Put a teaspoonful of filling on dough to the edge. Cover with another 3-inch round cookie and press edges together to seal; a fork works well. With a sharp knife, cut slits across the top. Sprinkle tops very lightly with sugar. Bake in 350-degree oven for 8 to 10 minutes or until light brown.

To make pineapple filling, mix sugar, flour, and reserved pineapple juice in saucepan until smooth. Stir in rest of ingredients and slowly cook until thick. Cool. Fill cookies.

Makes about 4 dozen cookies.

Featured on the cover.

Grandma's Rolled Molasses Cookies

1	cup molasses	1³/₄	teaspoons baking powder
¹/₂	cup shortening	1	teaspoon salt
1	teaspoon baking soda	1¹/₂	teaspoons ginger
2¹/₄	cups flour		

Cook molasses to boiling point. Remove from heat and add shortening and baking soda. Blend in dry ingredients. Chill dough 1 hour. Roll dough thin to ¹/₈-inch thick and cut with a 2¹/₂-inch round cutter or other desired shape. Place on lightly greased cookie sheet and bake in 350-degree oven for 6 to 7 minutes.

Watch closely! Because these cookies are dark, it is sometimes difficult to tell when they are overbrowned.

Makes 5¹/₂ to 6 dozen cookies.

WHITE SUGAR COOKIES

1	cup margarine or butter, softened	$1/2$	teaspoon almond extract
$1^1/2$	cups powdered sugar	$2^1/2$	cups flour
1	large egg	1	teaspoon baking soda
$1^1/4$	teaspoons vanilla	1	teaspoon cream of tartar

Cream butter and powdered sugar until light and fluffy. Add egg, vanilla, and almond extract. Blend in dry ingredients. Chill at least 1 hour. Roll $1/3$ of dough on floured pastry cloth or board. Cut in favorite shapes, sprinkle with granulated or colored sugar, and place on a lightly greased cookie sheet. Bake in 350-degree oven for 8 to 10 minutes. Roll dough thin for crisp cookies and bake for 6 to 7 minutes. Repeat with remaining dough.

Here's a short-cut method: Using heaping teaspoonfuls of dough, make balls and place on greased cookie sheet. With the flat bottom of a glass dipped in sugar, flatten cookies. Quick and easy perfectly shaped sugar cookies!

Makes $5^1/2$ to 6 dozen 2-inch cookies.

Featured on the cover.

CREAM COOKIES

Cookies:
 1   egg
 1/2 cup sugar
 1/2 cup whipping cream
 13/4 cups flour
 1/2 teaspoon salt
 11/2 teaspoons baking powder

Icing:
 1   cup powdered sugar
 1/2 teaspoon almond extract
 2   tablespoons milk
 1/8 teaspoon salt
      Red food coloring

To make cookies, beat egg and sugar until light and fluffy; blend in cream. Add flour with baking powder and salt. Mix well. Chill dough 1 hour. Roll dough to 1/4-inch thickness on a floured cutting board. Cut into 2-inch squares. With a knife, make two 1/2-inch indentations on each side of each square. Bake on greased baking sheet in 350-degree oven for 8 to 10 minutes or until set but not brown. Cool completely. Frost with pink-tinted icing.

To make icing, combine powdered sugar, almond extract, milk, salt, and a few drops of red food coloring. Mix all ingredients until smooth and spread on cooled cookies.

Makes 3 to 31/2 dozen cookies.

1993

GRANDMA CORRIGAN'S IRISH SWEET BISCUITS

1/2	cup butter	1/4	cup fine granulated sugar
11/2	cups flour		Sugar to sprinkle on top

Cut butter into flour and fine sugar to make a shortcrust pastry. Roll into ball and knead lightly. Roll dough 1/4-inch thick on a floured board and cut with 21/2-inch cutter. Place on an ungreased cookie sheet and sprinkle with sugar. Bake in 350-degree oven about 15 minutes or until lightly browned. Remove at once and cool. Serve with fruit, compotes, or ice cream.

Makes 21/2 to 3 dozen cookies.

ITALIAN FANS

1982

2/3	cup butter	2	cups flour
3/4	cup sugar	11/2	teaspoons baking powder
1	egg		
1/2	teaspoon grated orange rind	1/4	teaspoon salt
			Sugar to sprinkle on top
1/2	teaspoon vanilla		
4	teaspoons milk		

Cream butter and sugar until light and fluffy. Beat in egg, orange rind, vanilla, and milk. Blend in dry ingredients. Divide dough into 4 equal pieces and chill 1 hour. Roll each piece into 1/8-inch thick circles on floured board. Cut each circle into 8 pie-shaped wedges. Mark each wedge lightly with blade of knife to make lines that radiate from center to outside, resembling an open fan. Sprinkle with sugar. Place cookies 2 inches apart onto greased cookie sheets. Repeat with remaining dough. Bake in 375-degree oven for 8 to 10 minutes or until lightly browned.

Makes 32 to 36 cookies.

Greek Sesame Seed Twists

Gold Excellence Award Winner–Washington County Fair

1	cup butter	4	cups flour
1³/₄	cups sugar	2	teaspoons baking powder
2	eggs	¹/₂	teaspoon salt
²/₃	cup toasted sesame seeds, divided	¹/₄	cup water

Cream butter, sugar, and eggs until fluffy. Stir in ¹/₃ cup sesame seeds. Blend in dry ingredients, alternating with water. Chill dough for 2 hours. Roll dough on lightly floured board into rectangle ¹/₈-inch thick. Cut dough in 2x1-inch strips. Press one entire side of each strip in dish with remaining sesame seeds. Fold one end over at right angle to other, making bowknot effect. Bake on greased cookie sheet 2 inches apart in 350-degree oven for 8 to 10 minutes or until lightly browned. Remove immediately to cooling rack.

Makes 8 to 9 dozen cookies. *Featured on the cover.*

Honey Lemon Butter Cookies

1	cup butter	1	teaspoon lemon juice
1	cup honey	4	cups flour
1	egg, separated	1	teaspoon baking powder
1	tablespoon grated lemon rind	³/₄	cup chopped almonds

Cream butter and add honey in a fine stream. Beat in egg yolk, lemon rind, and lemon juice. Gradually add flour and baking powder. Stir in almonds. Chill 1 hour. Shape dough into small balls and arrange onto a greased cookie sheet 2 inches apart. Brush lightly with beaten egg white. Bake at 350-degrees for 10 to 15 minutes.

Makes about 4 dozen cookies.

GREEK EASTER COOKIES

Gold Excellence Award Winner–Washington County Fair

1	cup butter	2	cups flour
1/3	cup sugar	1	teaspoon baking powder
2	egg yolks		Whole cloves for top of each cookie
1/2	teaspoon rum extract		Powdered sugar for dusting
1	teaspoon vanilla		

Cream butter and sugar; add egg yolks, rum extract, and vanilla. Blend in flour and baking powder. Shape dough into small balls about 3/4-inch diameter or in shapes formed in 2-inch-long half-moons. Place cookies on lightly greased baking sheet 2 inches apart. Before baking, place a whole clove on top of each cookie and press down lightly. Bake in 350-degree oven for 10 to 12 minutes or until cookies are set but not browned. Let stand 2 minutes before removing from baking sheet. When cool, place on waxed paper and dust with powdered sugar. Because of the cloves, store these cookies separately.

Makes 7 to 8 dozen cookies.

Featured on the cover.

DANISH ALMOND TWISTS

2	cups unblanched almonds	1	egg, beaten
2	cups flour	1/2	teaspoon almond extract
1/2	cup sugar	2	teaspoons vanilla
1/2	teaspoon salt		Powdered sugar for dusting
3/4	cup butter		

Grate almonds. Combine flour, sugar, salt, and grated almonds in mixing bowl. Cut in butter with pastry blender until mixture resembles coarse crumbs; stir in combined egg, almond extract, and vanilla. Work dough with hands to form a ball. Roll level teaspoonfuls of dough on floured board with palm of hand to size of 4-inch pencil; form rings, overlapping ends. Place 3 inches apart onto ungreased cookie sheets. Bake in 350-degree oven 12 to 15 minutes. Dust powdered sugar over cooled cookies with a flour sifter.

Makes 7 to 8 dozen cookies.

CANDY CANE CHRISTMAS COOKIE
Gold Excellence Award Winner–Washington County Fair

Cookie:
- 1   cup margarine, softened
- 1   cup powdered sugar
- 1   egg
- 1 1/2   teaspoons almond extract
- 1   teaspoon vanilla
- 2 1/2   cups flour
- 1   teaspoon salt
- 1/2   teaspoon red food coloring

Topping:
- 1/2   cup sugar
- 1/2   cup crushed peppermint candy

Cream margarine and powdered sugar until fluffy. Beat in egg, almond extract, and vanilla. Stir in flour and salt. Divide dough in half and add red food coloring to one half. Roll two 4-inch strips, using 1 teaspoon dough from each color. Roll each on lightly floured board until smooth. Put strips side by side and press together, then twist like a rope and shape into candy canes. Form one cookie at a time. Place cookies 3 inches apart on an ungreased cookie sheet and bake in 375-degree oven for 7 to 9 minutes or until lightly browned. Remove cookies to a cooling rack and while still warm, sprinkle with mixture of crushed candy and sugar.

Make sure you store these Christmas cookies separate from the other kinds you make as the peppermint will affect the other cookies.

Makes about 4 dozen cookies.

Featured on the cover.

CREAM CHEESE COOKIES

1 cup margarine, softened
1 3-ounce package cream cheese, room temperature
1 cup sugar
1 egg, slightly beaten
1 tablespoon lemon juice
1 teaspoon grated lemon rind
2 1/2 cups flour
1 teaspoon baking powder

Blend margarine and cream cheese; beat in sugar until light and fluffy. Add egg, lemon juice, and rind; blend well. Blend in flour and baking powder. Chill dough for 1 hour. Force dough through cookie press onto an ungreased baking sheet, placing cookies 2 inches apart. Bake in 350-degree oven for 8 to 10 minutes or until lightly browned. Remove immediately from cookie sheet and cool completely.

Makes about 5 dozen cookies.

GRANDMA TORZEWSKI'S POLISH BUTTER "COOKIE"

1 cup butter
1 cup sugar
1 egg, separated
1 teaspoon vanilla
2 cups flour
1/2 teaspoon salt
1/3 cup finely chopped walnuts

Beat butter and sugar until fluffy. Add egg yolk and vanilla. Stir in flour and salt. Press dough in ungreased jelly roll pan, 15x10x1 inches, and spread the top with beaten egg white. Sprinkle with walnuts. Bake in 375-degree oven 20 to 25 minutes until golden brown. Cool and cut into 1x3-inch strips.

Makes 50 bars.

CHOCOLATE BROWNIES

4	ounces unsweetened chocolate	1¹/₂	cups flour

4 ounces unsweetened chocolate
²/₃ cup margarine
2 cups sugar
4 eggs
¹/₂ teaspoon vanilla

1^1/$_2$ cups flour
1 teaspoon baking powder
1 teaspoon salt
^{3}/$_4$ cup chopped walnuts, optional

Over low heat, melt chocolate and margarine. Beat in sugar, eggs, and vanilla. Add dry ingredients and combine, then add nuts, if desired. Pour into greased 9x13x2-inch pan and bake in 350-degree oven for 30 to 35 minutes or until no imprint remains when touched. Cool. Cut into squares or bars. While the brownies I won a blue ribbon for were not frosted, the frosting below is one my family especially likes on brownies.

Makes 12 to 16 squares.

Featured on the cover.

Frosting, optional:
1 ounce unsweetened chocolate
1 tablespoon margarine
1 cup powdered sugar
2 tablespoons hot water

Melt unsweetened chocolate and margarine. Add powdered sugar and hot water. Stir until smooth, adding a few more drops of water, if necessary. Spread on cooled brownies and let frosting set before cutting.

CHIP BARS

Gold Excellence Award Winner–Washington County Fair

Bottom Crust:
- 1/3 cup margarine, softened
- 1/2 cup brown sugar, packed
- 1 cup flour

Filling:
- 2 eggs, beaten
- 1 cup brown sugar, packed
- 1 teaspoon vanilla
- 2 tablespoons flour
- 1 teaspoon baking powder
- 1/2 teaspoon salt
- 1 cup semi-sweet chocolate chips
- 1 cup chopped walnuts or pecans
- Powdered sugar for dusting

To make bottom crust, mix all ingredients and press into bottom of ungreased 9x13x2-inch pan. Bake 10 minutes in 350-degree oven. Remove from oven.

To make filling, mix eggs and all dry ingredients. Add chips and nuts. Pour over hot crust and return to oven for 20 minutes. Cool and cut into bars or squares. Dust with powdered sugar.

Makes 12 to 16 bars.

Featured on the cover.

HOLLAND'S JAN HAGEL

1 cup butter	$1/2$ teaspoon cinnamon
1 cup sugar	1 tablespoon water
1 egg, separated	$1/2$ cup very finely chopped walnuts
2 cups flour	

Beat butter, sugar, and egg yolk until light and fluffy. Stir in flour and cinnamon. Pat into lightly greased jelly roll pan, 15x10x1 inches. Beat water and egg white until frothy; brush over dough with pastry brush. Sprinkle with nuts. Bake 20 to 25 minutes or until very lightly browned. Cut immediately into finger-like strips, 1x3 inches.

Makes 50 bars.

Frosted Honey Carrot Bars

Bars:

1 1/4 cups vegetable oil
1 1/2 cups honey
4 eggs
2 cups grated carrots
2 cups flour
2 teaspoons baking soda
1 teaspoon salt
1 1/2 teaspoons cinnamon
1 cup chopped walnuts

Frosting:

1 8-ounce package cream cheese, softened
1/3 cup honey
1 teaspoon vanilla

To make bars, blend together oil, honey, eggs, and carrots. Stir in dry ingredients and walnuts. Spread in a greased jelly roll pan, 15x10x1 inches. Bake in 350-degree oven for 20 to 25 minutes. Cool completely.

To make frosting, combine cream cheese, honey, and vanilla. Beat until smooth and easy to spread. Frost cooled bars.

Makes 24 to 36 bars.

DATE HONEY BARS

Bars:
- $1/2$ cup margarine
- 1 cup honey
- 1 teaspoon vanilla
- $1/4$ teaspoon salt
- $1 1/4$ cups oatmeal
- $1 1/2$ cups flour
- $1/2$ teaspoon baking soda

Date Filling:
- $1/4$ cup boiling water
- $1/2$ cup chopped dates
- $1/3$ cup honey
- $1/2$ cup coarsely chopped walnuts

To make bars, cream margarine and add honey in a fine stream. Add vanilla and blend in dry ingredients. Spread half of dough in greased 9x9x2-inch pan and spread filling over dough. Top with remaining dough dropped by teaspoonfuls on the top. Bake 30 minutes at 350 degrees or until golden brown. When cool, cut into 1x3-inch bars.

To make filling, pour boiling water over chopped dates in blender and let stand for 10 minutes. Add honey and walnuts. Blend all for 1 minute. Cool.

Makes 16 to 18 bars.

Featured on the cover.

HONEY PINEAPPLE BARS

1/2 cup margarine	1 cup flour
1/4 cup honey	1/2 teaspoon baking soda
1 egg	1/4 teaspoon salt
1 8-ounce can unsweetened, crushed pineapple with juice	1/4 teaspoon nutmeg
1 cup oatmeal	1/4 cup chopped pecans

Cream margarine and add honey in a fine steady stream. Beat well. Add egg, pineapple, and juice. Mix in dry ingredients and pecans. Pour into greased 9x9x2-inch pan and bake in 350-degree oven for 30 to 35 minutes or until golden brown. When cool, cut into squares or bars.

Makes 16 to 20 bars.

FRUIT AND HONEY BARS

2 tablespoons butter	1 1/4 cups whole wheat flour
1/4 cup honey	1 cup shredded coconut
2 eggs	3/4 cup chopped cashew nuts
1 tablespoon orange juice concentrate	1 15-ounce can crushed pineapple with juice
1 teaspoon vanilla	

Cream butter and add honey in a fine stream. Add eggs and beat well. Add orange juice concentrate and vanilla. Stir in flour a little at a time, and add coconut, cashews, pineapple, and juice. Mix well. Pour into a greased 9x13x2-inch pan and bake in 350-degree oven for 45 minutes or until nicely browned. Cool completely before cutting into squares or bars.

Makes 24 to 36 bars.

BREADS

Bread

Bread is a food made by mixing wheat flour, or other ground grain, and salt with water, milk, yeast, shortening, and sugar; the mixture is baked usually after kneading and shaping into loaves, rounds, or rolls.

The mention of "bread" brings to mind a good substantial food as well as a few phrases we use in daily conversation: bread winner, bread and butter, break bread. No matter how it is used in conversation, people know "bread" doesn't only mean food; it can often refer to something that is solid and basic.

In the late 1800's, when my grandmothers were baking bread, things seemed to be different. They made basic, no-frill breads to feed the hungry families. My mother's parents were originally from Krakow, Poland and my grandmother Torzewski's recipe went like this: "1 piece of yeast, cup of warm potato water, spoon of lard, pinch of salt, dab of sugar and flour necessary." Well, you get the general idea. Not much fuss, just basic down-home bread. She probably measured the lard by her spoon and the flour by her hand! She must have done a lot of basic bread baking for her family of twelve.

According to my mom, for a simple variation, her mother would "pinch off" pieces of plain white yeast bread dough just after the first rising, fry it in about 1/4-inch of fat in a frying pan, and sprinkle it with white sugar. This was eaten warm. The family usually didn't have a lot of sweets, so this must have been a real treat! This is what my mother said they called "quick bread," simply because it was made "quickly" and the bread did not go through the whole rising and shaping process.

My Irish grandmother Corrigan did make the traditional white yeast bread, but mostly she made baking powder biscuits and the traditional Irish soda bread. These have a heavy texture, nothing like the raised yeast bread in weight, looks, or taste. But that's what the Irish mostly ate with their vegetables. When we have store-bought white bread so readily available, it is difficult to imagine eating breads made with baking powder or baking soda most of the time.

My mother baked yeast white bread every week while I was growing up and has a recipe she has adapted through many years of baking. I work mostly with quick breads but do make products with yeast. You must experiment a little and find the recipe that works for you, but keep on working with it until you feel comfortable using it. No smell can compare with the heady aroma of baking homemade white bread. It simply cannot be duplicated!

I don't really recall when I first started baking, but I do remember working with bread dough when I was about six or seven years old. I had one of those aluminum bake sets for children that had several layer cake pans, miniature muffin cup pan, and a few 3x5-inch cookie sheets. I even had a tiny rolling pin. I would pester my mother to give me a bit of dough whenever she was baking bread so that I could make biscuits too. Well, I'd work my little hands until they cramped, rolling the dough, adding flour, re-rolling the dough and adding more flour, then forming tiny biscuits to put on the tiny baking sheet. By that time, the dough had a grayish hue from so much handling and added flour. My mom would bake those sorry looking "pebble" biscuits in her oven and then I'd try to "pawn" them off on the family. Needless to say, they were so hard my brothers, Mark and Pat, could have used them for ammunition for their sling-shots!

QUICK BREADS

Probably my favorite bread to make is the quick bread. I've developed a number of recipes and my "tasters" generally agree that quick breads taste great and are pretty easy to make. Actually, some quick breads taste more like a cake or dessert because of the high sugar content. My dad used to sample all my quick breads, and he usually ate them as a dessert. His favorite was my apple quick bread. Probably the best known of all quick breads is the traditional nut bread and banana bread.

Quick breads use a chemical agent such as baking powder or baking soda as a leavening instead of yeast. They need an acid, such as milk, sour cream, or buttermilk, to work. These breads are baked as soon as the batter is mixed. They are so named because they are speedily prepared compared to yeast breads. For light and tender muffins or bread with a gently rounded top, stir the batter JUST enough to moisten the ingredients. The batter will be lumpy. But remember if you overmix, you will cause toughness and tunnels. You can mix a batch of muffins from scratch in less than five minutes! In this age of doing everything quickly, this type of bread fits right in for many in-a-hurry homemakers who still want to bake for their families.

Quick breads of all kinds make great gifts, especially at Christmas and Easter time, and they are always good sellers at bake sales.

MY TIPS FOR MAKING QUICK BREADS AND MUFFINS

1. When making quick breads and muffins, gather all utensils, ingredients, and baking pans before you start. Turn oven on to preheat to temperature stated in recipe.

2. To prepare bread pan or muffin-cup pan, grease and flour or lightly coat with a cooking spray (spray shortening). Be careful not to spray too much or it will scorch the outside of your product. For best results, use the pan size called for in your recipe! Paper liners around muffins are unacceptable in competition and take away from the intended look of the well-formed muffin.

3. Work quickly putting the ingredients together, especially when mixing the batter. DO NOT OVERMIX! The batter should be lumpy. If you overmix, the result will be tunnels or holes inside the bread or muffins and tops that are high and pointed. The texture will be coarse and will not look as good as they can.

4. If you add dried fruit to the batter, "plump" the fruit first. To plump, soak dried fruit in warm water for about 5 minutes and then drain well before adding to the batter. Since dried fruit can take the moisture out of the batter, plumping the fruit will keep the bread moist.

5. Before putting your muffins or quick bread in the preheated oven, drop the pan, yes, drop it, several times from about 12 inches above the counter! This will help bring air bubbles to the surface of the batter so they can't be trapped inside, causing tunnels or holes.

6. Bake in preheated oven for time specified in the recipe. Tops should be nicely browned and the bread or muffins should test done when a wooden pick inserted in center comes out clean. Muffins especially seem to lose their brown color when cooled, so be sure they are done. A crack on top is traditional in quick breads; it is the leavening agent at work. Make sure the "crack" is also baked.

7. Quick breads can be frozen but they have a tendency to be drier. The best way to freeze quick breads is to put the warm bread in the refrigerator to cool completely, then wrap it for the freezer. This way condensation from the warm bread's steam won't get caught in the plastic bag or container and cause loss of quality. To thaw, put the bread in the refrigerator from the freezer and defrost unopened. This way your bread won't become soggy. Frozen breads are not the highest quality, so I do not recommend entering them in fair competition.

NATURAL INGREDIENT QUICK BREAD

1	egg, beaten	1	cup whole wheat flour
1/2	cup honey	3	teaspoons baking powder
1/2	cup vegetable oil	1/2	teaspoon cinnamon
3/4	cup milk	1	teaspoon salt
1/2	teaspoon vanilla	3/4	cup chopped nuts
1	cup white flour		

Blend egg, honey, oil, milk, and vanilla. Add flours, baking powder, cinnamon, and salt. Stir in nuts. Do not overmix! Grease and flour or coat with spray shortening a 9x5x3-inch loaf pan. Pour batter into pan and bake in 325-degree oven for 1 hour 15 minutes or until it tests done when wooden pick inserted in center comes out clean. Cool 10 minutes. Remove from pan and cool completely before slicing.

Makes 1 loaf.

NUT BREAD

3/4	cup sugar	3	cups flour
2	tablespoons vegetable oil	3 1/2	teaspoons baking powder
1	egg	3/4	teaspoon salt
1 1/2	cups milk	1 1/4	cups chopped walnuts or
1	teaspoon vanilla		nuts of your choice

Thoroughly mix sugar, oil, egg, milk, and vanilla. Stir in flour, baking powder, salt. Add nuts. Do not overmix! Grease and flour or coat with spray shortening a 9x5x3-inch loaf pan. Pour batter into pan and bake in 350-degree oven for 1 hour or until it tests done when wooden pick inserted in center comes out clean. Cool 10 minutes. Remove from pan and cool completely before slicing.

Makes 1 loaf.

MAPLE NUT BREAD

2	tablespoons vegetable oil	2 1/2	cups flour
1	cup sugar	3	teaspoons baking powder
3	tablespoons brown sugar	3/4	teaspoon salt
1	cup milk	1	cup coarsely chopped
1	egg, beaten		walnuts
1 1/2	teaspoons maple extract		

Mix oil, sugars, milk, egg, and maple extract. Add flour, baking powder, and salt. Blend in walnuts. Do not overmix! Grease and flour or coat with spray shortening a 9x5x3-inch loaf pan. Pour batter into pan and bake in 350-degree oven for 1 hour or until bread tests done when wooden pick inserted in center comes out clean. Cool 10 minutes. Remove from pan and cool completely before slicing.

Makes 1 loaf.

BANANA BREAD

1	egg	1	cup ripe, mashed bananas
2¹/₂	tablespoons vegetable oil	3	cups flour
1	cup sugar	3¹/₂	teaspoons baking powder
³/₄	cup milk	1	teaspoon salt
¹/₂	teaspoon vanilla	1	cup chopped walnuts

Beat egg with fork. Mix in oil, sugar, milk, vanilla, and bananas. Add flour, baking powder, and salt. Stir in nuts. Do not overmix! Grease and flour or coat with spray shortening a 9x5x3-inch loaf pan. Pour batter into pan and bake in 350-degree oven for 60 to 65 minutes or until it tests done when wooden pick inserted in center comes out clean. Banana bread tends to have the traditional crack on top of the bread; that's ok! Just make sure you bake the bread long enough so the crack is completely baked. Cool 10 minutes. Remove from pan and cool completely before slicing.

Makes 1 loaf.

Featured on the cover.

PUMPKIN BREAD

1/2	cup margarine, softened	1	teaspoon baking soda
1 1/2	cups sugar	1/4	teaspoon baking powder
1	egg	1	teaspoon cinnamon
1/3	cup water	3/4	teaspoon salt
1	cup pumpkin	2/3	cup chopped walnuts
1 3/4	cups flour		

Mix margarine, sugar, egg, and water. Stir in pumpkin and mix well. Add flour, baking soda, baking powder, cinnamon, and salt. Add walnuts and stir only enough to moisten flour. Grease and flour or coat with spray shortening a 9x5x3-inch loaf pan. Pour batter into pan and bake in 350-degree oven for 1 hour or until it tests done when wooden pick inserted in center comes out clean. Cool 10 minutes. Remove from pan and cool completely before slicing.

Makes 1 loaf.

APPLESAUCE QUICK BREAD

2 1/2	tablespoons vegetable oil	1/2	cup grated green apple
1 1/4	cups sugar	1 1/2	cups flour
2	tablespoons brown sugar	3/4	teaspoon baking soda
2	eggs, slightly beaten	1/4	teaspoon baking powder
2 1/2	teaspoons vanilla	1 1/4	teaspoons cinnamon
3/4	cup sweetened applesauce	3/4	teaspoon salt

Mix oil, sugars, and eggs. Add vanilla, applesauce, and grated apple. Blend in flour, baking soda, baking powder, cinnamon, and salt. Do not overmix! Grease and flour or coat with spray shortening a 9x5x3-inch loaf pan. Pour batter into pan and bake in 350-degree oven for 1 hour or until it tests done when wooden pick inserted in center comes out clean. Cool 10 minutes. Remove from pan and cool completely before slicing.

Makes 1 loaf.

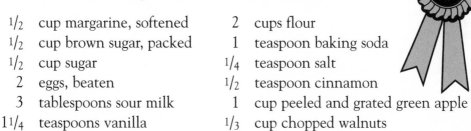

APRICOT NUT BREAD

1	cup sugar	3	cups flour
2	tablespoons vegetable oil	3^1/$_2$	teaspoons baking powder
1	egg	^{1}/$_4$	teaspoon cinnamon
^{3}/$_4$	cup milk	1	teaspoon salt
^{3}/$_4$	cup orange juice	^{1}/$_4$	cup chopped walnuts
^{1}/$_2$	teaspoon orange extract	1	cup finely chopped dried apricots

Mix sugar, oil, egg, milk, orange juice, and extract well. Blend in flour, baking powder, cinnamon, and salt. Add nuts and apricots. Do not overmix! Grease and flour or coat with spray shortening a 9x5x3-inch loaf pan. Pour batter into pan and bake in 350-degree oven for 60 to 70 minutes or until it tests done when wooden pick inserted in center comes out clean. Cool 10 minutes. Remove from pan and cool completely before slicing.

Makes 1 loaf. *Featured on the cover.*

APPLE QUICK BREAD

1985

^{1}/$_2$	cup margarine, softened	2	cups flour
^{1}/$_2$	cup brown sugar, packed	1	teaspoon baking soda
^{1}/$_2$	cup sugar	^{1}/$_4$	teaspoon salt
2	eggs, beaten	^{1}/$_2$	teaspoon cinnamon
3	tablespoons sour milk	1	cup peeled and grated green apple
1^1/$_4$	teaspoons vanilla	^{1}/$_3$	cup chopped walnuts

Mix margarine, sugars, eggs, milk, and vanilla. Stir in flour, baking soda, salt, and cinnamon. Add grated apple and nuts. Do not overmix! Grease and flour or coat with spray shortening a 9x5x3-inch loaf pan. Pour batter into pan and bake in 350-degree oven for 55 to 60 minutes or until it tests done when wooden pick inserted in center comes out clean. Cool bread 10 minutes. Remove from pan and cool completely before slicing.

Makes 1 loaf.

CHERRY NUT BREAD

1/4	cup margarine, softened	3	teaspoons baking powder
1/2	cup sugar	1/2	teaspoon baking soda
1/2	cup brown sugar, packed	1	teaspoon salt
2	eggs	1	cup chopped pecans
1	cup sour milk	1/3	cup chopped maraschino
1/4	cup maraschino cherry juice		cherries, well-drained
21/2	cups flour		

Combine margarine and sugars. Add eggs, sour milk, and cherry juice. Stir in flour, baking powder, baking soda, and salt. Mix quickly; fold in pecans and cherry pieces, but don't overmix! Grease and flour or coat with spray shortening a 9x5x3-inch loaf pan. Pour batter in pan and bake in 350-degree oven for 60 to 65 minutes or until it tests done when wooden pick inserted in center comes out clean. Cool 10 minutes. Remove from pan and cool completely before slicing.

Makes 1 loaf.

CRANBERRY NUT BREAD

Gold Excellence Award Winner–Washington County Fair

1/4	cup margarine, softened	1 1/2	teaspoons baking powder
1	cup sugar	1/2	teaspoon baking soda
3/4	cup orange juice	3/4	teaspoon salt
1 1/4	teaspoons orange extract	2	cups chopped fresh cranberries
1	egg	3/4	cup chopped nuts
2	cups flour		

Mix margarine, sugar, juice, extract, and egg. Add flour, baking powder, baking soda, and salt. Stir in cranberries and nuts just until moistened. Grease and flour or coat with spray shortening a 9x5x3-inch loaf pan. Pour batter into pan and bake in 350-degree oven for 1 hour or until it tests done when wooden pick inserted in center comes out clean. Cool 10 minutes. Remove from pan and cool completely before slicing.

Makes 1 loaf.

Featured on the cover.

CRANBERRY-PINEAPPLE BREAD

1/4 cup margarine, softened	2 1/2 teaspoons baking powder
1 cup brown sugar, packed	1/4 teaspoon baking soda
2 eggs	1/2 teaspoon salt
1 8-ounce can crushed pineapple with juice	1 cup chopped fresh cranberries
2 cups flour	3/4 cup chopped pecans

Cream margarine, brown sugar, and eggs until fluffy. Add pineapple and juice. Blend in flour, baking powder, baking soda, and salt. Stir in cranberries and pecans. Grease and flour or coat with spray shortening a 9x5x3-inch loaf pan. Pour batter into pan and bake in 350-degree oven 50 to 60 minutes or until it tests done when wooden pick inserted in center comes out clean. Cool 10 minutes. Remove from pan and cool completely before slicing.

NOTE: Buy cranberries in the fall when they are a good purchase, then freeze them just as they come from the store, using double plastic bags.

Makes 1 loaf.

PINEAPPLE QUICK BREAD

1/4 cup margarine, softened	2 cups flour
3/4 cup brown sugar, packed	2 1/2 teaspoons baking powder
1/4 cup sugar	1/4 teaspoon baking soda
2 eggs	1/2 teaspoon nutmeg
1 8-ounce can crushed pineapple with juice	1/2 teaspoon salt
	1 cup chopped walnuts

Mix margarine, sugars, and eggs well. Stir in pineapple and juice. Add flour, baking powder, baking soda, nutmeg, and salt. Add walnuts. Don't overmix! Grease and flour or coat with spray shortening a 9x5x3-inch loaf pan. Pour batter into pan and bake in 350-degree oven for 1 hour or until bread tests done when wooden pick inserted in center comes out clean. Cool 10 minutes. Remove from pan and cool completely before slicing.

Makes 1 loaf.

ORANGE-BLUEBERRY QUICK BREAD

1	egg	3	cups flour
1	cup sugar	3½	teaspoons baking powder
2	tablespoons vegetable oil	½	teaspoon cinnamon
¾	cup milk	1	teaspoon salt
¾	cup orange juice	¾	cup chopped nuts
1	teaspoon orange extract	1	cup blueberries, fresh or frozen

Beat egg in bowl with fork. Add sugar and oil. Mix in milk, orange juice, and orange extract. Add flour, baking powder, cinnamon, and salt. Add nuts and blueberries. Mix only until flour is moistened. Don't overmix! Grease and flour or coat with spray shortening a 9x5x3-inch loaf pan. Pour batter into pan and bake in 350-degree oven for 60 to 70 minutes or until bread tests done when wooden pick inserted in center comes out clean. Cool 10 minutes. Remove from pan and cool completely before slicing.

Makes 1 loaf.

1985

ORANGE PRUNE BREAD

1	cup pitted prunes	$1/2$	cup orange juice
	Water to cover prunes	$2 1/4$	cups flour
2	eggs	$1 1/2$	teaspoons baking powder
3	tablespoons vegetable oil	$1/4$	teaspoon cinnamon
1	cup sugar	$3/4$	teaspoon salt
1	tablespoon grated orange peel	$3/4$	cup chopped nuts
1	teaspoon orange extract		

Cover prunes with water and cook until tender. Drain and reserve $1/2$ cup prune water. Cool prunes, then dice. In a bowl, beat eggs slightly with fork and add oil, sugar, orange peel, extract, reserved prune water, and orange juice. Mix in flour, baking powder, cinnamon, and salt. Add nuts and diced prunes. Stir only enough to moisten. Grease and flour or coat with spray shortening a 9x5x3-inch loaf pan. Pour batter in pan and bake in 350-degree oven for 55 to 60 minutes or until it tests done when wooden pick inserted in center comes out clean. Cool 10 minutes. Remove from pan and cool completely before slicing.

Makes 1 loaf.

Featured on the cover.

MIXED FRUIT QUICK BREAD

1	cup mixed dried fruit	$1/2$	cup orange juice
	Water to cover fruit	$21/2$	cups flour
1	cup sugar	3	teaspoons baking powder
3	tablespoons vegetable oil	$1/2$	teaspoon cinnamon
2	eggs, slightly beaten	1	teaspoon salt
1	teaspoon orange extract	$3/4$	cup chopped nuts

Cover fruit with cold water and cook until soft, about 10 minutes. Drain, reserving $1/2$ cup liquid. Cool. Mix sugar, oil, eggs, extract, orange juice, and reserved liquid from mixed fruit. Add flour, baking powder, cinnamon, and salt. Add nuts. Do not overmix! Grease and flour or coat with spray shortening a 9x5x3-inch loaf pan. Pour batter into pan and bake in 350-degree oven for 60 to 70 minutes or until it tests done when wooden pick inserted in center comes out clean. Cool 10 minutes. Remove from pan and cool completely before slicing.

Makes 1 loaf.

1991

WHOLE WHEAT MUFFINS

1	egg	1	cup flour
1	cup milk	1	cup whole wheat flour
1/4	cup vegetable oil	2 1/2	teaspoons baking powder
1/2	cup sugar	1	teaspoon salt
2	tablespoons brown sugar	1/2	teaspoon ground cinnamon
1/2	teaspoon vanilla		

In a bowl, beat egg with a fork and add milk, oil, sugars, and vanilla. Stir in flours, baking powder, salt, and cinnamon. Stir just enough to moisten. The batter will be lumpy, but don't overmix! Grease and flour muffin cups or coat with spray shortening. Pour batter into cups, filling two-thirds full. Bake in 350-degree oven for 20 to 25 minutes or until golden brown.

Makes 12 muffins.

1980

RASPBERRY MUFFINS

1	egg	2 1/2	teaspoons baking powder
1/2	cup milk	1/4	teaspoon salt
1/4	cup vegetable oil	1/2	cup fresh raspberries, broken up
1/2	cup sugar		if large, or frozen and not thawed
1 1/2	cups flour		

In a bowl, beat egg with a fork and stir in milk and oil. Add sugar, flour, baking powder, and salt, and stir just enough to moisten the flour. Stir in raspberries, but don't overmix! The batter will be lumpy. Grease and flour muffin cups or coat with spray shortening. Pour batter into cups, filling two-thirds full. Bake in 350-degree oven for 20 minutes or until golden brown. Cool 10 minutes, then remove from muffin cups.

Makes 12 muffins. *Featured on the cover.*

STREUSEL TOPPED COFFEE CAKE

Coffee Cake:
- 2 cups flour
- 1 cup sugar
- 3 teaspoons baking powder
- 3/4 teaspoon salt
- 1/3 cup butter, softened
- 1 large egg
- 1/2 cup milk
- 1/2 cup sour cream
- 1 1/2 teaspoons vanilla

Streusel Topping:
- 1/3 cup brown sugar, packed
- 1/4 cup white sugar
- 1 teaspoon cinnamon
- 1/2 cup finely chopped walnuts

To make coffee cake, blend flour, sugar, baking powder, and salt. Add butter, egg, milk, sour cream, and vanilla. Beat well for 2 minutes. Grease and flour or coat with spray shortening a 9x9x2-inch pan. Pour batter into pan and cover with streusel topping. Bake in 350-degree oven for 35 to 40 minutes or until it tests done when wooden pick inserted in center comes out clean.

To make topping, combine sugars, cinnamon, and walnuts. Sprinkle on top of coffee cake before baking.

Makes 9 to 12 squares.

Featured on the cover.

COFFEE CAKE WITH BAKED-ON TOPPING

Coffee Cake:
- 1/4 cup margarine, softened
- 3/4 cup sugar
- 1 egg
- 1/2 teaspoon vanilla
- 1/2 cup milk
- 1 1/2 cups flour
- 2 1/4 teaspoons baking powder
- 1/2 teaspoon salt

Topping:
- 2 tablespoons margarine, softened
- 1/4 cup brown sugar
- 2 tablespoons flour
- 1 teaspoon cinnamon
- 1/2 cup chopped nuts

To make coffee cake, mix margarine, sugar, egg, vanilla, and milk. Stir in dry ingredients. Do not overmix! Grease and flour 9x9x2-inch pan. Spread in batter, then sprinkle on topping. Bake in 350-degree oven for 30 to 35 minutes.

To make topping, combine margarine, brown sugar, flour, cinnamon, and nuts. Sprinkle on top of coffee cake dough before baking.

Makes 9 to 12 squares.

BAKING POWDER DOUGHNUTS

2	eggs	4	teaspoons baking powder
1	cup sugar	1/4	teaspoon cinnamon
4	tablespoons melted shortening	1/4	teaspoon nutmeg
1	cup milk	1/2	teaspoon salt
4	cups flour		Oil for frying

Beat eggs well. Beat in sugar, shortening, and milk. Add flour, baking powder, cinnamon, nutmeg, and salt. Beat with electric mixer until smooth. Turn part of dough onto generously floured cutting board. Roll to 1/3-inch thick. Cut dough with sharp floured doughnut cutter. Let rest 1 minute. Drop in 4 inches of oil that has been heated to 380 degrees. Fry doughnuts a few at a time; do not crowd. Turn doughnuts as they rise to surface, frying a total of 2 to 3 minutes or until golden brown. Lift from oil with long fork. Drain on absorbent paper towel. Repeat with remaining dough. Serve doughnuts plain or coat with powdered sugar, sugar and cinnamon, or frost with white or chocolate icing.

Makes about 2 1/2 dozen 3-inch doughnuts.

Featured on the cover.

CAKES

Cakes

A cake is a mixture of flour, eggs, milk, sugar, and extract that is baked and often covered with icing. Because you work with a finely balanced formula of ingredients, you must measure correctly, follow directions carefully, and use the right size pan. Your success will be measured in the final product. A nicely baked and frosted cake is not only pretty to look at, it's a sweet ending to any meal and a compliment to the cook!

There are two types of cakes we all are familiar with: butter cakes and foam cakes. Cakes made with solid shortening, butter, or margarine are called butter cakes. Some butter cakes we all know are yellow, white, chocolate, and spice cakes.

The second type of cake is the foam cake. The best known foam cakes are angel food, sponge, and chiffon cakes. It is the foam of beaten egg whites that is the primary leavening agent and gives the cake the light open texture.

Frosting is the "crowning glory" to top off all your hard work. When you become skilled in making basic frosting, you will be able to create with decorations, colors, and flavors. Decorated cakes have helped mark the milestones of our lives, like birthdays, graduations, weddings, anniversaries, and any other special occasion. Because I took cake decorating classes, I was able to supply the family with attractive cakes for almost every occasion. It's a nice hobby and can be profitable.

Thinking back to when I started making cakes, one particular incident comes to mind. I had put a lot of effort into a dark, moist chocolate cake. After mixing the ingredients and baking it, I let it cool and then I frosted it with a rich, dark chocolate frosting. I cut the cake and artfully placed the pieces on a serving plate.

My brothers' friend, Dave, was at our house and stayed for lunch. After the usual sandwiches were eaten, my mother put the plate of cake pieces on the table for dessert. Well, Dave eyed the cake with interest, reached for a piece and took a huge bite. From the look on his face it certainly was pleasing to his taste buds! By this time I was beaming with pride for a job well done when out of nowhere and to no one in particular, my brother Dick asked who made the cake. My mother answered that I did. With a very straight face, and quick hand, Dave promptly put the bitten piece of cake back on the plate. He teasingly wanted to see the surprise on my face! After the group was thoroughly entertained, they proceeded to consume every last piece of cake on the plate! This is not the only time something like that happened. My brothers and their friends constantly teased me during those years I was learning to bake, especially when I began to make all sorts of "creations" like tortes and other desserts! They still seem to enjoy razzing me about my baking even though whatever I bake and bring to family gatherings seems to disappear quickly enough!

MY TIPS ON MAKING BUTTER CAKES

1. Read and follow the recipe exactly! Don't substitute items in the recipe and use the exact amount specified.

2. Gather the ingredients you will be using. Most ingredients mix better at room temperature. When using the best ingredients, your end product will be the best quality. Baking powder controls much of the height, grain, and texture of the cake. Use the exact amount given in recipes. Baking powder and soda deteriorate unless kept tightly closed in a cool, dry place; remember to buy them fresh before making your fair entries.

    Shortening counteracts the toughening ingredients in a cake and helps to improve the texture and distribute flavor. Use the type of shortening specified in the recipe for best results.

    Flour provides the basic structure that holds cake ingredients together. Cake flour is very high quality flour milled especially for delicate cakes. All-purpose flour is fine for breads, biscuits, and pastries or for cakes that have a sturdier texture. Again, use the type of flour the recipe calls for.

    Use the freshest milk, eggs, and nuts, too. If the recipe calls for sour cream or buttermilk, use the commercial kind; it works best. Also, remember that eggs separate best when cold, but beat up lighter when at room temperature.

3. Gather all the utensils you will need.

4. Preheat the oven to the temperature specified in the recipe. It's better to make the oven wait for the cake than make the cake wait for the oven!

5. Always use the correct size cake pan, the one called for in the recipe. When making a butter cake, make sure the pan isn't too large or your cake will be flat, and if the pan is too small or shallow, the cake will bulge over and lose its shape. Don't fill cake pans more than half full. Layer pans should be at least $1^1/_2$ inches deep; square or oblong pans should be 2 inches deep; pound cake or loaf pans should be at least 3 inches. Shiny metal pans are good for cake baking because they reflect heat away from the cake and produce a light, brown tender crust. Grease bottoms and sides of pans well then dust with flour and shake out the excess, or coat pans lightly with spray shortening.

6. There are two ways to mix the ingredients for a butter cake. The first is to combine flour and other dry ingredients into the bowl. Then add the liquid and short-

ening, beating until well blended. Next add eggs and beat again for several minutes. My mom uses the second method, creaming the shortening and sugar until it is fluffy and then adding the liquid and flour alternately until well blended, adding the eggs last. Either way works fine but it's best to use the method specified in the recipe.

7. Divide the batter evenly into prepared pans and bake with the rack in the middle of the oven. Stagger layer pans and keep slightly apart so they bake evenly. When the minimum baking time is up, test the cakes. Touch cakes in center lightly and if no imprint remains, the cake is done. Or test by inserting a wooden pick in center; if it comes out clean, the cake is done. Cool completely before removing from pan.

8. To make smooth frosting, use sifted powdered sugar.

My Tips On Making Foam Cakes

1. Read your recipe carefully and gather all ingredients, utensils, and pans you will need. Preheat oven to the temperature called for in your recipe.

2. For foam cakes DO NOT grease the pan. The batter must cling to the side and tube of the pan in order to rise properly. Also to cool properly, the cake must stay in the pan when inverted.

3. Separate eggs while cold and let whites warm to room temperature before beating to get the best volume.

4. Using rubber scraper, carefully push batter into tube pan. Carefully cut through batter with knife to prevent large air holes.

5. Bake as recipe directs, until no imprint remains when cake is lightly touched in center. Immediately hang the cake pan upside down over a funnel or bottle until it's cold, then remove cake from pan.

My Tips For Freezing and Storing Cakes

1. Butter and foam cakes can be stored nicely under a cake cover, which protects your frosting and helps to keep the cake moist. Even though you can store your cakes this way, it doesn't prevent them from disappearing!

2. Almost any cake freezes well. Just make and bake as usual. If unfrosted, the cake will keep better, up to six months. The convenience of plastic containers makes it easy to store and freeze cakes. When you are ready to use, just thaw at room temperature.

POUND CAKE

7	large eggs	$^1/_4$	teaspoon baking soda
$^1/_4$	teaspoon salt	$1^1/_2$	cups margarine, softened
$1^1/_4$	teaspoons cream of tartar	$2^1/_2$	tablespoons lemon juice
$2^1/_3$	cups sugar, divided	2	tablespoons plus 1 teaspoon
$2^1/_2$	cups flour		vanilla
			Powdered sugar for dusting

Separate eggs and let stand at room temperature. Beat egg whites in a large mixing bowl on high speed until frothy. Add salt and cream of tartar. Gradually add 1 cup sugar and beat until soft peaks form. Set aside.

In a large mixing bowl, combine remaining sugar, flour, and baking soda. Mix at low speed. Blend in margarine, lemon juice, and vanilla. Add egg yolks, one at a time, until well blended. Gently fold the beaten egg white mixture into cake batter. Grease and flour or coat with spray shortening a tube pan or two 9x5x3-inch loaf pans. Pour batter into pans and bake in 325-degree oven for 90 minutes. Turn off oven and leave cake in oven 15 minutes longer. Cool on rack for 15 minutes more, then remove from pan and finish cooling thoroughly. Before serving, dust with powdered sugar.

Makes 16 to 20 servings.

WHITE CAKE
(Low Cholesterol)

1¹/₂ cups cake flour
1 cup sugar
2 teaspoons baking powder
¹/₂ teaspoon salt

¹/₃ cup low cholesterol stick margarine
(not whipped)
²/₃ cup skim milk
1 teaspoon vanilla
2 small egg whites

Blend flour, sugar, baking powder, and salt. Add margarine, milk, and vanilla. Beat for 2 minutes. Add egg whites and beat for 2 minutes longer, scraping sides and bottom of bowl often. Grease and flour or coat with spray shortening an 8x8x2-inch square pan. Pour batter into pan and bake in 350-degree oven for 30 minutes or until it tests done when wooden pick inserted in center comes out clean. Cool completely and serve with fruit or yogurt.

Makes 9 servings.

FROSTED MARBLE CAKE

Cake:

2 cups cake flour
1 1/4 cups sugar
2 1/2 teaspoons baking powder
1 teaspoon salt
1/3 cup shortening
1 cup milk, divided
1 teaspoon vanilla
1 egg
1 ounce unsweetened chocolate, melted and cooled
1/4 teaspoon baking soda
2 tablespoons water

Butter Frosting:

1/3 cup margarine, softened
3 to 4 tablespoons milk
3 cups powdered sugar
2 teaspoons vanilla
1/4 teaspoon salt

To make cake, sift flour, baking powder, and salt together. Add shortening, 2/3 cup milk, and vanilla. Beat 2 minutes, scraping sides and bottom of bowl. Add remaining milk and egg. Beat 2 minutes more. Pour half the batter into another bowl and add melted chocolate, baking soda, and water. Beat this mixture for 30 seconds. Grease and flour or coat with spray shortening two 8-inch layer cake pans. Spoon white and chocolate batter alternately into pans. Run a knife through batter to give marbled effect. Bake in 350-degree oven 30 to 35 minutes or until cake tests done when wooden pick inserted in center comes out clean. Cool completely and frost with butter frosting.

To make butter frosting, combine margarine, milk, powdered sugar, vanilla, and salt. Beat all ingredients in small bowl, adding more milk, if necessary, until frosting is smooth and easy to spread.

Makes 10 to 12 servings.

Featured on the cover.

1989

One-Layer Chocolate Cake

3/4	cup flour	3/4	cup milk	
1	cup sugar	1/2	teaspoon vanilla	
1	teaspoon baking powder	1	egg	
1/8	teaspoon baking soda	2	ounces unsweetened chocolate,	
1/2	teaspoon salt		melted and cooled	
2	tablespoons shortening			

Mix flour, sugar, baking powder, baking soda, and salt. Add shortening, milk, and vanilla and beat for 2 minutes with electric mixer. Add egg and chocolate and beat 2 minutes more, scraping sides and bottom of bowl often. Grease and flour or coat with spray shortening a 9x9x2-inch pan for a flatter cake, or a 8x8x2-inch pan for a higher cake. Pour batter into pan and bake in a 350-degree oven for 30 to 35 minutes or until it tests done when wooden pick inserted in center comes out clean. Cool completely and frost with your favorite chocolate frosting.

Makes 9 to 12 servings.

BANANA CAKE

Cake:

1 1/2 cups cake flour
1   cup sugar
2   teaspoons baking powder
1/2   teaspoon salt
1/3   cup margarine, softened
2/3   cup mashed bananas
1/4   cup milk
1   egg

Sweetened Whipping Cream (optional):

1   cup cold whipping cream
1/2   teaspoon vanilla
2   tablespoons powdered sugar

To make cake, mix flour, sugar, baking powder, and salt. Add margarine, mashed bananas, and milk. Beat 2 minutes. Add egg and beat 2 more minutes. Grease and flour or coat with spray shortening an 8x8x2-inch pan. Pour batter into pan and bake in 350-degree oven for 30 minutes or until wooden pick inserted in center comes out clean. Cool completely and frost with your favorite frosting. You may also frost the cake with sweetened whipped cream. Slice fresh bananas on top to complete the dessert.

To make sweetened whipped cream, chill the bowl and beaters. Place whipping cream, vanilla, and powdered sugar in the bowl. Beat until stiff, 2 to 3 minutes. Makes 2 cups.

Makes 9 servings.

Honey White Cake

1/4	cup margarine	6	tablespoons milk
1/4	cup sugar	3/4	teaspoon vanilla
1/3	cup honey	1/4	teaspoon almond extract
12/3	cups cake flour	2	egg whites
1/2	teaspoon salt	1/4	teaspoon cream of tartar
2	teaspoons baking powder		

Cream margarine and sugar. Add honey in a fine stream and beat until light and fluffy. Sift flour, salt, and baking powder together. Add dry ingredients and milk, alternately, to the creamed mixture. Add vanilla and almond extract. In a small bowl, beat egg whites and cream of tartar until they hold their shape. Fold egg white mixture gently into cake mixture. Grease and flour or coat with spray shortening an 8x8x2-inch pan. Pour batter into pan and bake in 350-degree oven for 30 minutes or until cake tests done when wooden pick inserted in center comes out clean. Cool completely and frost with your favorite frosting.

Makes 10 to 12 servings.

Vanilla Honey Cake

1/2	cup margarine	1/2	teaspoon salt
1	cup honey	2	teaspoons baking powder
2	eggs	1/2	cup milk
2	cups flour	11/2	teaspoons vanilla

Cream margarine and add honey in a fine stream. Add eggs one at a time, beating well after each addition. Sift flour, salt, and baking powder together and add alternately with milk to creamed mixture. Add vanilla. Grease and flour or coat with spray shortening two 8-inch layer cake pans. Pour batter into pans and bake at 350-degrees for 30 to 35 minutes or until cake tests done when wooden pick inserted in center comes out clean. Cool and frost with desired frosting.

Makes 10 to 12 servings.

LEMON HONEY CAKE

1/2 cup shortening	1/2 teaspoon salt
1 cup honey	2 tablespoons lemon juice
2 eggs	1/4 cup milk
2 cups cake flour	1 teaspoon grated lemon peel
3/4 teaspoon baking soda	

Cream shortening. Add honey in a fine stream while continuing to beat. Add eggs and beat well. Sift flour, baking soda, and salt together. Add lemon juice to milk. Add combined dry ingredients, alternating with milk mixture, to creamed mixture. Stir in lemon peel. Grease and flour or coat with spray shortening two 8-inch layer pans. Pour batter into pans and bake in 325-degree oven for 25 to 30 minutes or until cake tests done when wooden pick inserted in center comes out clean. Cool completely and frost with your favorite lemon flavored frosting.

Makes 10 to 12 servings.

ORANGE HONEY CAKE

$1/2$ cup margarine	$1 1/2$ teaspoons baking powder
$1/2$ cup sugar	$1/4$ teaspoon salt
$1/2$ cup honey	$1/4$ cup milk
1 large egg	$1/4$ cup orange juice
$1/2$ teaspoon orange extract	
1 cup plus 2 tablespoons cake flour	

Cream margarine and sugar until fluffy. Add honey in a fine stream and continue beating. Add egg and orange extract. Combine cake flour, baking powder, and salt, and add alternately with milk and juice to creamed mixture. Blend well. Grease and flour or coat with spray shortening an 8x8x2-inch pan. Pour batter into pan and bake in 350-degree oven for 25 to 30 minutes. Cool completely.

This cake is sweet, so, if desired, just dust a small amount of powdered sugar on top before serving; no other frosting is necessary.

Makes 9 servings.

WHITE CUPCAKES

2	cups flour	1/2	cup shortening, softened
1 1/2	cups sugar	1	cup milk
3	teaspoons baking powder	1 1/2	teaspoons vanilla
1	teaspoon salt	2	eggs

Mix flour, sugar, baking powder, and salt. Add shortening, milk, and vanilla to dry ingredients. Beat 2 minutes, scraping sides and bottom of bowl often. Add eggs and beat 2 minutes longer. Line muffin tins with paper baking cups and fill cups half full. Bake in 350-degree oven for 18 to 20 minutes. Cool completely and frost with your favorite frosting or use as a base for shortcake.

Makes 18 small cupcakes.

CHOCOLATE CUPCAKES

1 1/4	cups flour	4	tablespoons shortening
1 1/3	cups sugar	1	cup milk
1 1/4	teaspoons baking powder	3/4	teaspoon vanilla
1/4	teaspoon baking soda	1	egg
1/4	teaspoon salt	3	ounces unsweetened chocolate, melted and cooled

Blend flour, sugar, baking powder, baking soda, and salt. Add shortening, milk, and vanilla. Beat 2 minutes, scraping sides and bottom of bowl. Add egg and chocolate and beat 2 more minutes. Line muffin tins with paper baking cups and fill cups half full. Bake in 350-degree oven for 18 to 20 minutes. Cupcakes should have a nice rounded top. Cool completely and frost with your favorite chocolate frosting.

Makes 18 small cupcakes.

CHOCOLATE CHIFFON CAKE

Gold Excellence Award Winner–Washington County Fair

Cake:
- $1/2$ cup cocoa
- 1 cup boiling water
- $13/4$ cups cake flour
- $13/4$ cups sugar
- $11/2$ teaspoons baking soda
- $3/4$ teaspoon salt
- $1/2$ cup vegetable oil
- 8 eggs, separated
- $21/2$ teaspoons vanilla
- $1/2$ teaspoon cream of tartar

Chocolate Glaze:
- $1/3$ cup margarine
- 2 cups powdered sugar
- 2 ounces unsweetened chocolate, melted and cooled
- 2 to 4 tablespoons hot water

To make cake, stir cocoa in boiling water until smooth. Cool 20 minutes. Mix flour, sugar, baking soda, and salt in bowl. Make a well in center and add in order: oil, egg yolks, cocoa mixture, and vanilla. Beat with spoon until smooth. Beat egg whites and cream of tartar in large bowl until stiff peaks form. Gradually pour egg yolk mixture over egg whites and mix, gently folding with rubber scraper just until blended. Pour batter into ungreased tube pan and bake in 325-degree oven for 60 to 65 minutes. Cool, remove from pan, and frost with chocolate glaze.

To make chocolate glaze, melt margarine; add powdered sugar and chocolate. Add water a little at a time until glaze is smooth and easy to spread.

Makes 12 to 16 servings.

Featured on the cover.

CANDY

CANDY

This is the sweetest section of my book—the candy recipes! A definition of candy or confectionery is "processed food based on a sweetener, which may be sugar or honey and to which other ingredients such as flavorings, spices, nuts, fruits, milk products, or chocolate have been added."

Candy making, or sugar cookery, truly is an "art." It involves working with sugar and liquid over controlled heat, watching the temperature closely as it reaches different stages, and handling the syrup so you end up with the kind of candy you want.

My mom always made sweets for us: divinity, taffy, caramel corn, and fudge at Christmas time. Candy making is special, and making sweet treats for family and friends in the form of homemade candy takes time and effort on your part. But everyone can enjoy the results of your hard work.

Homemade candy is probably made the most at Christmas time, but I think candy is a big part of every special occasion: birthdays, anniversaries, Valentine's Day, Easter, and any other gathering. Candy is also a nice way to say thank you or a way to give a personal gift. There are very few people who do not like candy in one form or another. My mom always made sea foam candy, a "sister" of divinity, for us to take to school bake sales, but she made sure there was a little left at home for us too! Nothing says it better than homemade candy!

By the time everyone took a piece of candy in my family, quite a bit of it was gone, so I really didn't have to worry about what to do with candy that didn't turn out all that well. But I had to put up with a lot of grumbling about the fact that it didn't taste like mom's! My first attempt at fudge, for Christmas many years ago, was a disaster! I guess I just didn't follow the basic directions very closely because it turned out sugary. I probably stirred it too soon and then not enough, two very important points to watch when making fudge. I know now that if you beat it before it cools down, it will be grainy or sugary and if you stop beating it too soon, the fudge will not be creamy. Fudge I make now has come from years of practice.

I remember other treats I tried to make when I was young. One Sunday afternoon, I was pestering my mom to make caramel corn. But mom was busy with something else, so she said if I wanted caramel corn that bad I should make it myself! Well, I was about 12 years old at the time and my younger brother, Pat, was again my co-conspirator in this adventure. We had watched my mother make caramel corn many times, and of course, we both thought we knew the best way to make it. So I decided to make the caramel and Pat was to pop the corn. He finished his job and I was earnestly working at cooking when he got bored and left. I kept at it until I thought the caramel was just right, or so I thought, then poured it over the popped corn. Well, Pat came around in time to help with the finished product. We tried to pick it up but the caramel corn stuck to our hands, the bowl, our hair, our clothes, the table, to just everything! It didn't have a bad taste, but what a mess!

As the family came to investigate what we were up to in the kitchen, they tried the caramel corn that still was in the bowl, but nobody could chew it, not even the dog! It stuck to our teeth! I really don't know what I did to that batch of caramel corn, but mom said she'd make sure she would be around the next time we attempted to make caramel corn! She told us that even though it didn't turn out as well as we hoped, the main thing was that we tried.

Candy sweetened with honey has a distinctive flavor. The very mild, all natural clover honey works well with any honey candy recipe. Usually the lighter the color the milder the honey. Honey has a slightly higher calorie count but usually tastes sweeter than sugar, so you use less and end with about the same calories as when you use sugar. Use a honey candy recipe or substitute honey for sugar in your favorite candy recipes.

MY TIPS ON MAKING CANDY

1. Follow the candy recipe EXACTLY. Recipes may contain variations of rules so follow the recipe carefully if you want your candy to be perfect.

2. Use a heavy, deep pan that has straight sides and is large enough to let the sugar syrup boil freely.

3. Cook candy by stirring it until the sugar dissolves and comes to a boil, then stir ONLY to prevent scorching.

4. Wipe off any sugar crystals that form on the sides of the pan with a wet cloth. This helps prevent grainy candy.

5. When the mixture starts to boil, put a candy thermometer in the pan, covering the bulb but not touching bottom of pan. Being sure you've reached the right temperature is a very important part of your candy making. Buy a good candy thermometer or test syrup with the cold water method like my mother taught me to use. This method is simple, but it tells a great deal about how the syrup is cooking. To use this method, drop a small amount of hot syrup into a clear measuring cup filled with very cold water and see what stage the syrup has reached.

The Soft Ball Stage (234 to 240 degrees): syrup can be picked up but it doesn't stay in ball shape; for making fudge.

The Firm Ball Stage (242 to 248 degrees): firm ball is made from drop but if water is stirred, the ball falls apart; for making caramels.

The Hard Ball Stage (250 to 268-degrees): drop turns into a hard ball but it's still workable; for divinity.

The Soft Crack Stage (270 to 290 degrees): syrup forms a thread instead of a ball; for making butterscotch.

The Hard Crack Stage (300 to 310 degrees): syrup forms brittle threads that break easily; for making hard candy.

DIVINITY CANDY

2¹/₄	cups sugar	2	egg whites
¹/₃	cup white corn syrup	1¹/₂	teaspoons vanilla
¹/₂	teaspoon salt	1	cup chopped walnuts
¹/₃	cup water		

In heavy 2-quart saucepan, put sugar, corn syrup, salt, and water. Stir and cook over high heat until sugar is dissolved. Keep cooking until it reaches the hard ball stage, 255 degrees on candy thermometer. Make sure you wipe off the sugar crystals that form on the sides of the pan. Beat egg whites until stiff and pour the hot syrup slowly over the beaten egg white, beating until candy fluffs up. Add vanilla and continue beating on medium speed of electric mixer until mixture begins to lose its gloss and a small amount dropped from a spoon holds soft peaks. Stir in nuts. If candy is too stiff for your mixer, finish beating by hand. Be patient; beating may take as long as 15 minutes!

Drop candy by teaspoonfuls onto waxed paper, but you must work quickly because the mixture will harden. Add a few drops of hot water to candy if it starts to set before you're finished. You can also pour candy into a buttered 8x8x2-inch pan, to be cut into squares when cold.

Makes about 1 pound.

Featured on the cover.

BROWN SUGAR DIVINITY

1	cup light brown sugar, packed	2/3	cup water
1	cup sugar	2	egg whites
1/3	cup light corn syrup	1 1/2	teaspoons vanilla
1/2	teaspoon salt	3/4	cup chopped nuts

Put brown sugar, sugar, corn syrup, salt, and water in a heavy 2-quart saucepan. Bring mixture to a boil over medium heat, stirring constantly. Make sure you wipe off any sugar crystals that form on the sides of the pan. Boil until it reaches the hard ball stage, 265 degrees on candy thermometer. Before syrup reaches temperature, beat egg whites until peaks form. Continue beating syrup and slowly pour in a fine stream into egg whites; beat until mixture loses its gloss. Stir in vanilla and nuts. If candy is too stiff for your mixer, finish beating by hand. Be patient; beating may take as long as 15 minutes!

Drop candy by teaspoonfuls onto waxed paper, but you must work quickly because the mixture will harden. Add a few drops of hot water to candy if it starts to set before you're finished. You can also pour candy into a buttered 8x8x2-inch pan, to be cut into squares when cold.

Makes about 1 pound.

OLD FASHIONED BUTTERSCOTCH

Gold Excellence Award Winner–Washington County Fair

2¼   cups sugar
⅓   cup light corn syrup
½   cup butter
2½   tablespoons water
2   tablespoons vinegar

In a heavy 2-quart saucepan, combine all ingredients and cook over medium heat until sugar is dissolved. Continue cooking, stirring only when you need to control foaming or to avoid sticking. Wipe off any sugar crystals that form on the sides of pan and continue cooking to hard crack stage, 300 degrees on candy thermometer. Let stand 1 minute. Working quickly, drop by teaspoonfuls onto a baking sheet covered with foil. Make patties about 1 inch in diameter. Or pour mixture onto buttered foil, let cool, and break into pieces. If mixture thickens, set the pan in hot water until it's workable.

For the fair, I dropped the mixture in small amounts into the cups of a buttered mini-muffin tin. After the mixture cooled, I just popped out the pieces.

Makes about 1¼ pounds.

Featured on the cover.

HONEY PEANUT BUTTER SQUARES

$1/2$ cup honey
1 cup peanut butter
$11/2$ cups nonfat dry milk powder
$1/2$ cup crushed cereal or coconut
24 peanut halves

Mix honey and peanut butter together. Stir in milk powder and mix well. Pour in buttered 8-inch square pan and chill well. Cut into squares or roll into balls and coat with crushed cereal or coconut. Press a nut half on top of each piece.

Makes 24 pieces.

HONEY CARAMEL SQUARES

1 teaspoon flour
$1/4$ teaspoon salt
$1/4$ cup evaporated milk
2 tablespoons melted butter

$1/2$ cup honey
$1/2$ teaspoon vanilla
$1/2$ cup chopped walnuts

Combine flour, salt, and milk in a saucepan. Mix in butter and honey. Place over heat, stirring constantly, and cook to firm ball stage, 258 degrees on candy thermometer. Remove from heat and stir in vanilla and walnuts. Pour into buttered 8x8x2-inch pan. Chill well. Cut into squares.

Makes about 20 pieces.

Honey Pecan Rolls

2	teaspoons flour	1	cup honey
1/2	teaspoon salt	1/2	teaspoon vanilla
1/4	cup evaporated milk	1	cup chopped pecans
4	teaspoons butter, melted	1	cup mini-marshmallows

Combine flour, salt, and milk in saucepan. Mix in butter and honey. Cook over high heat, stirring constantly, to firm ball stage, 258 degrees on candy thermometer. Remove from heat and quickly stir in vanilla. Place layer of pecans in the bottom of a buttered 9x9-inch pan. Cover pecans with 1/4-inch hot caramel mixture. Cover with marshmallows. Cover marshmallows with remaining caramel mixture. Cut into strips 1 inch wide and 2 inches long and shape into rolls. Wrap each roll in waxed paper. Chill.

Makes about 24 pieces.

Featured on the cover.

1986

HONEY CHEWS

1/2 cup butter
1 cup honey
1/2 cup chopped dates
1 cup chopped nuts

Bring butter and honey to hard ball stage, 260 degrees on candy thermometer. Remove from heat and add chopped dates and nuts. Stir for 2 minutes, then pour into buttered 8-inch square pan. Cool and cut into squares. May be wrapped in waxed paper for storing.

Makes 24 pieces.

HONEY COCONUT BITES

1991

1/2 cup butter	1/2 teaspoon salt
2 tablespoons milk	1 cup grated coconut
1 cup flour	1 teaspoon vanilla
3/4 cup honey	2 cups crushed crisp rice cereal

Combine all ingredients except vanilla and cereal in a saucepan. Cook over medium heat, stirring constantly until dough leaves the sides of the pan and forms a ball. Remove from heat and cool. Add vanilla and cereal. Shape into 1-inch balls. May be rolled in additional coconut. Chill thoroughly.

Makes about 42 pieces.

HONEY DATE MORSELS

2	cups cornflakes	1	tablespoon butter
3/4	cup pitted dates	2	teaspoons lemon juice
1/2	cup chopped pecans	30	pecan halves
2	tablespoons honey		

Put cornflakes, dates, and chopped pecans through a grinder. Add honey, butter, and lemon juice to cereal mixture. Knead until well blended. Shape into small balls, top with pecan half, and chill.

Makes 30 pieces.

HONEY DATE BALLS

1/3	cup honey
3	tablespoons nonfat dry milk powder
1/2	cup ground dates, packed
1/2	cup finely chopped nuts
	Finely chopped nuts for rolling

Mix honey and dry milk powder until smooth. Add ground dates and nuts and mix well. Form into balls and roll in additonal finely chopped nuts. Chill.

Makes 24 small balls.

INDEX

About the Author

When Sue-Ann recalls childhood memories, it's of a warm home filled with the aroma of cooking and baking. She was born to hard working parents, Esther and Lawrence Corrigan, and grew up in the Milwaukee area with three brothers and one sister. She learned from early on how to make home-style foods for the family table and to produce the bakery needed to help feed the family of seven. This hands-on experience provided the foundation which helped to fine-tune her skills and enable her to move from the family kitchen to winning blue ribbons.

She is married to John, a steam fitter by trade, and has two children and two grandchildren. They have made their home in the Richfield, Wisconsin, area for over twenty-two years. Through the years she has been a Girl Scout Leader, Red Cross Volunteer, and continues to volunteer at her church. She worked part-time as office help and currently works in a local floral shop. She sings with the local Community Chorus and, along with John, attends auctions and goes to flea markets looking for collectibles.

Sue-Ann attended classes and seminars on food preparation, microwave cookery, cake decorating, and baking. She makes many tasty goodies but she really enjoys baking cookies of all kinds.

In her book, she shares her winning recipes and practical baking advice learned through years of experience while striving to make every one a winner!